# It's NOT That Complex!

Second Edition

# It's NOT That Complex!

Second Edition

©2015 by ICOM Multimedia

Author: Phil Yoder

Also available as a Kindle Book

www.itsnotthatcomplex.com

$14.95 USD

Publisher: ICOM Multimedia

ISBN: 978-0-9851022-4-1

Second Edition

9 780985 102241

Dedicated to the belief that common sense,
ethical behavior, and new individual
initiatives are required for
our society to survive

"The ideas I stand for are not mine.
I borrowed them from Socrates.
I swiped them from Chesterfield.
I stole them from Jesus.
And I put them I a book.
If you don't like their rules,
whose would you use?"
- Dale Carnegie

# Index

# Introduction

The purpose in writing *'It's NOT That Complex'* is based on the belief that Americans are abandoning their innate ability to form common-sense opinions and act on them as opposed to accepting popular perspectives from the media or others in their social or business circles. This 'abandonment' is subtle and regularly defended because it requires a certain amount of effort to step back, analyze issues, identify the *real* problems and simplify discussions. All too often we watch others debate symptoms and never insist on discussing the underlying problem(s). We passively accept the analysis of others and retreat into a zone of denial, believing that 'things can't be *that* bad'. We continue to live comfortably without understanding that a new level of proactive, vocal participation is necessary!

With the ever increasing number of information sources confronting us each day, determining which ones are credible and which ones are downright misleading can be an overwhelming task. Combined with the pressures of everyday tasks and responsibilities, it is far too easy to form beliefs and opinions without stopping to analyze which sources are relatively objective and which ones are downright self-serving. I say 'relatively' objective because few information sources are truly objective in that their mere existence often depends, to a certain extent, on promoting one viewpoint or another.

This book's organizational style was designed simply to allow a reader to pick and choose which topics are most relevant or important and read them in any order. The quotes included establish that the ideas I am promoting are not new or original. Most of them originated long ago from very intelligent folks. I have also avoided using specific current events or individuals as illustrations (which would have been very easy to do) in the interest of making this book applicable over a long period of time.

I will undoubtedly be accused of over-simplifying complex issues. While many of these topics may deserve a much longer dissertation, most do not benefit by lengthy debates that overly complicate simple, logical conclusions. My purpose is simply to encourage everyone to think, refuse to accept the opinions of the masses, and stand up for what is logical, right and sensible. It is the only way our country will find a new and productive direction.

Not a single idea or suggestion in this book is impractical or impossible to apply! In order to be implemented, the recommendations discussed require an open mind, considerable personal effort, and a willingness to accept change. The changes necessary will be painful for some short-term but very beneficial long-term for all. Our future prosperity and security are at stake!

Along with a recognition of these principles is the need for a new breed of leadership – leaders with common sense that are not afraid to speak to unpopular viewpoints and *sell* the obvious solutions to the masses.

The intelligence and fortitude of individual citizens *can* reorient our country and culture. The first step is to identify with these important principles – loudly and passionately!

When it doesn't make sense, don't let it stay that way

*"What luck for rulers that men do not think."*
*- Adolf Hitler*

13

"If you can't explain it simply, you don't understand it well enough!"
- Albert Einstein

# Accountability

*"It is not only what we do, but also what we do not do, for which we are accountable."*

*- Molière*

Accountability is simple . . . it means accepting responsibility for one's actions (or inactions) - and meeting one's obligations. Whether as an employee, a family member or a bureaucrat, common sense dictates that one's responsibilities and obligations be clearly understood and demonstrated in order to hold a job, an elected office or position of leadership. Only then can respect and credibility be earned.

It's criminal when elected officials demonstrate[1] no accountability to those who voted them into office. A few have gone so far as to state publicly that they know they are acting contrary to the wishes of their constituents but that they personally 'know best' what is good for all. They further seem unable to separate their 'job' obligations from their 'next-election-campaign' objectives. The result is that selfish interests and the issues of lobbyists and donors are the priorities pursued. Accountability vanishes.

This blatant conflict-of-interest needs to be clearly pointed out to all elected officials and a code of ethics developed as to what it means to 'represent' a constituency. Meanwhile, only a deluge of letters and calls (with a few recalls and impeachments along the way) has a chance at reversing this absurd trend.

---

[1] See **Actions Speak Louder Than Words!**

# Actions Speak Louder Than Words!

*"As I get older, I pay less attention to what men say,
I just watch what they do."*
- *Andrew Carnegie*

The strategy of '...*promise anything to get elected...*' adopted by many politicians, has become almost universal. Why don't we hold elected officials accountable for their commitments and promises? Do they not work for us?[2] Aren't they sworn to represent us? The average citizen seems all too content to shrug his or her shoulders and respond – 'Everyone running for office does it!'[3] Promises are made with absolutely no intent to follow through. Why accept this deceptive behavior? Would you live with someone, marry someone, or hire someone who repeatedly practiced this behavior?

As children, we were all taught the phrase **'Actions Speak Louder than Words'**. The wisdom contained in this phrase is indisputable. It is a simple way to determine someone's true character and, ultimately, how they value honesty. It's simple: with no honesty in business and government, our society is doomed to failure!

Persistently remind leaders of their promises! Ask hard questions. Insist on answers that makes sense! If you don't get real answers, broadcast their non-responsiveness and campaign against them. Actions are the final, indisputable proof of intent.

*"What you do speaks so loud that I cannot hear what you say."*
- *Ralph Waldo Emerson*

---

[2] See **Bureaucrats**
[3] See **Comparative Rationalization**

# Active Citizenship

*"Democracy is the most demanding of all forms of government in terms of the energy, imagination, and public spirit required of the individual."*
*- George C. Marshall*

Active citizenship refers to the idea that members of a society have roles and responsibilities as citizens even if they do not have formal positions in government. Active citizenship further includes a *requirement* that we exercise these responsibilities *because* we've been granted certain rights and freedoms.

The issue of rights vs. responsibilities[4] should not be minimized. With the 'right' to vote, we become responsible for those we elect. With the 'right' to enjoy our national infrastructure comes the responsibility to pay taxes[5]. The right to consume resources logically dictates our responsibility to conserve etc.

The next obvious step in this process is the responsibility to remove those leaders who do not exercise common sense, behave responsively and appropriately, or engage in dishonest practices. In private enterprise, under-performers, dishonest staff members, and unresponsive employees are terminated if they don't correct their ways. In public positions, our expectation should be no less.

Every citizen should be vocal about underperforming public officials at the very least - and thoroughly understand the process required to remove them when necessary.

---

[4] See **Rights vs. Responsibilities**
[5] See **Taxes**

# Advertising

*"What is the difference between unethical and ethical advertising?*
*Unethical advertising uses falsehoods to deceive the public;*
*ethical advertising uses truth to deceive the public."*
*-- Vilhjalmur Stefansson*

Needless to say, the business of advertising has evolved from an art form, supplemented by media technologies, into a highly sophisticated and calculated activity. Obviously, the goal is to attract purchasers of goods or services by whatever means is most productive and efficient. This sometimes results in deceptive and marginally ethical behavior which misleads prospective buyers or places them in awkward positions where emotional decisions are made under pressure.

The power of suggestion – whether 'savings' or other ego-boosting propositions, combined with 'painless' payment options often results in purchase decisions that are not prudent.

As consumers, we need to view all advertising with a skeptical eye, realizing that advertisers have 'their' selfish interests at heart – not your best interests! Read between the lines – if it sounds too good to be true, it probably is!

# Affirmative Action

*"Affirmative action is the attempt to deal with malignant racism by instituting benign racism."*
*- Elliott Larson*

Affirmative action policies, minority set-asides, and equal opportunity programs were originally intended to correct wrongful discrimination practices in the workplace, our educational institutions and government-sponsored programs. However, these initiatives and mandates have now created reverse discrimination – penalizing innocent members of the majority - under the distorted rationalization that two wrongs make a right!

Honest, deserving job candidates have been penalized while less deserving candidates are rewarded, advancing further the entitlement[6] mentality so pervasive in some segments of our culture. Further, applying a 'remedy' for historical 'wrongs' to citizens today makes about as much sense as imprisoning a descendent for the crimes of his great grandfather!

Don't misunderstand - discrimination on the basis of age, color, sex, religion etc. is wrong - and should remain illegal and punishable . . . but affirmative action programs are not fair or proper solutions.

Acting ethically and properly[7], while showing no favoritism or permitting any artificial advantage, is the only necessary mandate!

---

[6] See **Entitlement**
[7] See **Ethics, Right Thing**

# Arrogance

*"The truest characters of ignorance are vanity
and pride and arrogance."*
- *Samuel Butler*

There is a distinct line between self-confidence and arrogance . . . just as there is a clear difference between earning respect and demanding it[8]. Truly great and intelligent leaders understand this.

Leaders who routinely display pomposity, self-righteousness, and egotistical, superior attitudes usually have intellects and work ethics that are inversely proportional. The arrogant leader sees his personal agenda first – and assumes that his ideas are automatically the best while rarely giving consideration to other perspectives. Arrogance is often followed by narcissism, where the considered opinions and absolute knowledge of others is totally disregarded.

One who is committed and diligently works to truly solve problems has no time or need to pontificate before the press. Effective managers don't need to publicly announce their accomplishments - true accomplishments are observed. True leaders do not make excuses, knowing that their supporters don't need excuses and their detractors won't accept them anyway!

Arrogance and narcissism are negative personality traits and defining characteristics of individuals who should never be voted into positions of leadership!

---

[8] See **Respect**

# Attitude

*"Weakness of attitude becomes weakness of character"*
*- Albert Einstein*

Our attitudes reflect our opinions, beliefs, and knowledge. More importantly, they should direct our actions. When we voice our opinions and beliefs but fail to communicate them vigorously to leaders that can effect change, we are wasting time and energy.

As Albert Einstein said, this leads to '...weakness of character...'

Karl Meninger, the renowned psychiatrist said 'Attitudes are more important than facts' which explains why the average consumer listens to the media, co-workers and friends and often forms opinions without regard for factual verification. It explains why we are prone to believe politicians on the campaign trail when they echo what we want to hear.[9] Ultimately it explains why winning politicians are usually (but unfortunately) the ones who best articulate whatever the masses want to hear, regardless of their commitments and intentions.

Our belief systems are totally reflected in our attitudes – so we must be careful to conduct regular 'self-examinations' to make sure what we believe makes sense – and that our attitudes express a logical analysis of the subject matter in question.

Form your own beliefs through personal thought and analysis; express your attitudes with conviction - and follow through by intelligently contributing to change and communicating with those who can more directly effect change!

---

[9] See **Belief Systems**

# Austerity

*"You can't talk your way out of what you've behaved yourself into."*
*- Stephen R. Covey*

Austerity means '... rigorously self-disciplined, severely simple, and uncompromising...' As solutions go, solving difficult problems often requires sacrifice. Many of the issues facing our society have roots in the continuous prosperity experienced during our lifetimes. When economic and social challenges demand change – we often treat even the simplest of changes as radical demands contrary to what we 'deserve'.

What we 'deserve' often leads to an attitude of entitlement[10] and totally contradicts the concept of austerity. Austerity is as much an attitude as it is a practice or discipline. Austerity requires a change of attitude, a focus on new commitments and usually changes in some components of our lifestyle.

Solving our economic condition calls for a return to a society that produces and contributes – not a society where individuals focus on what they can 'take' from the system. Not only must individuals **believe** this but individuals must also contribute by **producing** something of value commensurate with what they expect to receive.

Focusing on one without the other will only perpetuate our economic and social decline.

*"That man is the richest whose pleasures are the cheapest."*
*- Henry David Thoreau*

---

[10] See **Entitlement**

# Bailouts

Bailing out a corporation in trouble due to a series of bad executive decisions with the money of taxpayers is not a solution.

The law of supply and demand in our free enterprise system is a 'natural law'[11] that cannot be altered or improved upon. Healthy competition has built our system into the strongest business environment in the world. History has presented us with multiple governing ideologies and concepts that attempted to modify, regulate, redefine and overrule this concept without success.

The current bailout fervor results from attempts to bypass this natural law *and* the refusal of business and political leaders to employ responsible and ethical practices. Believing that there exists an entity poised to 'rescue' failing cities, states or corporations will never encourage proper decision-making. No business or public entity is entitled to a reward for its failure to follow good business principles. No one understands this better than the small business entrepreneur who lives and dies by making hard decisions. Why should big business or governmental entities have a different experience?

Bailout programs for individuals or families are no different. They are simply ill-advised entitlement[12] programs!

Bailouts are never a good idea over the long term. They do nothing but promote irresponsibility! Insist that your legislative representatives embrace this concept and refuse to participate in any form of bailouts!

---

[11] See **Natural Laws**
[12] See **Entitlement**

# Belief Systems

*"If a man is offered a fact which goes against his instincts, he will scrutinize it closely, and unless the evidence is overwhelming, he will refuse to believe it. If, on the other hand, he is offered something which affords a reason for acting in accordance to his instincts, he will accept it even on the slightest evidence. The origin of myths is explained in this way."*

*- Bertrand Russell*

Why do you believe what you believe? Why do you act the way you act? Why do you defend what you defend?

What people believe to be true should be based on personal experiences, study and research, and private reasoning. Next, everyone is inevitably influenced by respected acquaintances who are 'believed' to be credible. Then - there are those unsolicited daily messages that bombard us that are easy to accept as true – without study, research or consideration of the source.

Unfortunately, once one develops a belief system about a given topic, his or her opinions and attitudes about that subject become less flexible. Facts even become less important. We all have difficulty being flexible or honest when faced with facts that contradict our beliefs. Honesty requires that we examine *exactly* why we do what we do, think what we think, and defend what we defend – and a search for truth! We should be prepared and willing to change our minds!

Develop your own belief system, rather than blindly accepting a popular one[13]. It's amazing how many folks never *independently* form a personal belief system!

---

[13] See **Unions**

# Big Picture

*"In the absence of clearly-defined goals,*
*we become strangely loyal to performing daily trivia*
*until ultimately we become enslaved by it. "*
*- Robert Heinlein*

From a management perspective, one personal characteristic valued above almost all others in an employee, is the ability of that employee to make decisions based on his or her understanding of the 'big picture' - in other words, understanding how their decisions will affect the overall enterprise, as-a-whole, over the long term.

In one's personal life, in politics, and in virtually all walks of life, one's intelligence, maturity, and likelihood-to-succeed is determined by one's understanding of the 'big picture'. Making day-to-day decisions with an understanding and sensitivity as to how that decision will impact everything else is crucial to success.

Of course, understanding the 'big picture' in a group setting involves identifying common goals – something that is often made more complex than necessary. If a group can't agree on common 'goals', it's obvious that the issue is being made far too complex!

If all leaders had a 'big picture' mentality, an understanding of their 'job' responsibilities, and an appreciation of the need for salesmanship [14] in their daily routines, the ineffectiveness and gridlock [15] in our government would disappear.

---

[14] See **Salesmanship**
[15] See **Gridlock**

# Blame

*"A man can fail many times, but he isn't a failure
until he begins to blame somebody else."*
*- John Burroughs*

Beware of folks who frequently use the words, 'it's not my fault' or 'I didn't do anything wrong', and blame others regularly for things that aren't right, acceptable or ideal. This is a simple but unmistakable indication that they accept no responsibility for their present circumstance. Repeatedly assigning blame or fault is a clear statement of one's obsessive need to be 'right' and a declaration that they can, obviously, do no wrong themselves.

One problem with this type of individual is that they will never be a contributing part of a productive team or an effective leader. There is an old adage . . . 'One is either part of the problem or part of the solution'. There is no middle ground. Many legislators and other elected officials spend a great deal of time assigning responsibility elsewhere rather than rolling up their sleeves and working on solutions.[16] Maturity and intelligence dictates that you work only on things that you can change, and refuse to focus on things of the past that can't be changed.

When you observe someone in a leadership position, whether public or private, that possesses this character flaw, either take action to remove them from that position or remove yourself from their 'jurisdiction' - things will not get better until you do!

*"When you blame others, you give up your power to change."*
*- Dr. Robert Anthony*

---

[16] See **Comparative Rationalization, Rhetoric**

# Budgets

*"The budget should be balanced, the Treasury should be refilled, public debt should be reduced, the arrogance of officialdom should be tempered and controlled, and the assistance to foreign lands should be curtailed lest Rome become bankrupt. People must again learn to work, instead of living on public assistance."*
*- Cicero - 55 BC*

Balancing a public budget is the equivalent of operating a business at the breakeven point – which is the absolute minimum criteria for survival. Anyone who embraces the delusion that operating a government entity or business indefinitely at a loss (i.e. deficit spending) is not qualified to be its leader! Since the beginning of civilization this concept has been true – and no current 'enlightenment' offers any plausible alternative. Why is this minimum standard not the basis for all spending discussions? Why are our bureaucrats permitted to employ these 'make-believe' solutions when so much intelligence exists among constituents'? Our deficit is the worst in history and getting worse by the day!

While on this subject, let's debunk the 'profit is a dirty word' myth. If you don't understand why profit is a good thing in *all* business environments, educate yourself![17] (And don't believe for a minute that government is not a business, subject to the same rules!) The current federal budgeting process is a Ponzi scheme! (which is illegal for the rest of us!) If your chosen public servants do not support the idea of having a mandatory balanced budget annually, impeach them immediately!

---

[17] See **Profit**

# Bureaucrats

*"You will never understand bureaucracies until you understand that for bureaucrats procedure is everything and outcomes are nothing."*
*- Thomas Sowell*

Bureaucrats also, unfortunately, do not derive their power from their intelligence, performance, or track records. So how do we replace bureaucrats with true representatives who are qualified?

First, we must somehow identify candidates with the appropriate motives for seeking public office and a proper understanding of their job description. Are they challenged by the tasks of governing or simply looking for personal enrichment or long term income security? Second, we must examine their qualifications. If they haven't successfully managed a business entity, they are simply not qualified! Third, look at their experience, track record and historical performance. A very defined set of business skills and 'people' skills is required. We can't afford to have amateurs in government! Our current executive and legislative branches would look very different if we followed these three guidelines.

Often our leaders are selected based on their oratory and speech-making abilities alone.[18] Today's bureaucrats seem to recognize only two tasks: getting elected and getting re-elected. Conflict-of-interest opportunities are rampant! When rational, ethical, productive performance and honest delivering on promises doesn't follow, a recall or impeachment process should be immediate!

*"Bureaucracy is a sickening beast for*
*people with innate common sense"*
*- Stan Otts*

---

[18] See **Specious Statements** and **Rhetoric**

Our current system offers too many opportunities to become personally enriched by serving special interests and too much incentive for a legislator to serve a minimum length of time only to be rewarded by a lifetime of benefits. Compromised ethics and character flaws immediately and dramatically develop. Whether term limits resolve this problem or not can be debated – but a rapid recall process, ethics mandates, and accountability conversations would be a huge beginning!

Legislation forcing our representatives to experience the same cultural and societal environments as the masses would also help - offering them the same health insurance and pension options; the same airport screening experiences; the same legal treatment for legal infractions, and only performance-based bonus opportunities.

When our elected representatives do not 'live' in the same world as those they represent, they cannot possibly do a good job as representatives of the people.

Elect representatives who understand that their primary job is to represent their constituents (not to be confused with lobbyists) while managing the business 'owned' by their constituents! Recall and replace them when they voice opinions that are clearly not representative, or violate good business practices.

*"Any change is resisted because bureaucrats have a vested interest in the chaos in which they exist."*
*- Richard Milhous Nixon*

# Capitalism

*"Capitalism demands the best of every man – his rationality – and rewards him accordingly. It leaves every man free to choose the work he likes, to specialize in it, to trade his product for the products of others, and to go as far on the road of achievement as his ability and ambition will carry him."*

*-Ayn Rand*

It's hard to imagine a more fair, efficient and self-regulating system than this. Almost like a natural law [19], the efforts of dictators, politicians and academicians to create a 'better' system have not resulted in any sustainable alternative.

One must ask then, what motivation do critics have in condemning capitalism? Two possibilities come to mind. First, those who are so unmotivated and/or lazy that they cannot understand the concept of self-determination will undoubtedly pursue a path of entitlement [20] indefinitely. Second, those who refuse to study history or analyze the alternatives see their individual roles as being powerless – or at best passive pawns in a system designed and controlled by trusted leaders.

When leaders begin imposing regulations in an attempt to improve on this system, we should all closely examine the true motives. While they often claim to be improving the 'system' for the good of all, the truth is usually aligned with a special interest group who has campaigned for special treatment. These actions should be exposed by honest media as unethical and counterproductive!

---

[19] See **Natural Laws**
[20] See **Entitlement**

# Change

*"Faced with the choice between changing one's mind
and proving there is no need to do so,
almost everyone gets busy on the proof."*
*- John Kenneth Galbraith*

It is human nature to resist change. Change forced upon us disrupts our routines, our expectations, our careers and our personal lives. Change is rarely welcomed but, at the same time, change is absolutely unavoidable.

Maturity, however, dictates how we deal with change . . . and whether we see change as opportunity or evil. The changes suggested in this book are all positive long-term – even if painful in the short term.

The challenge is for mature-minded leaders to put on their 'sales' hats and *sell* the need for specific changes to those they represent. This is not a task to take lightly, it is very necessary. Note that I said 'sell' . . . not 'cram it down their throats' in the dark of the night or from behind closed doors. The differences between good leaders and poor ones are often summed up in this simple practice. Great leaders *sell* change and *persuade* the masses; poor leaders use hollow statements, rhetoric, intimidation and subterfuge.

Pick leaders that have honorable objectives *and* are willing to use persuasion, not under-handed techniques, to achieve them.

*"All great change in America begins at the dinner table"*
*- President Ronald Regan*

# Change - For the Wrong Reasons

*"Much of the social history of the Western world, over the past three decades, has involved replacing what worked with what sounded good."*

*- Thomas Sowell*

Of course it 'sounds' good to be green, it 'sounds' good to remedy injustices, and it 'sounds' good to embrace politically correct phraseology[21] in our speaking. However, before jumping on these popular bandwagons, have we examined thoroughly the costs as compared to the benefits? Have we determined whether we are replacing one problem with another? Does it pass a reasonable 'common sense' test?

Far too many folks embrace popular 'movements' simply because it was suggested to them by advertising or the media and 'sounded' good - and totally fail to look at underlying issues. When businesses resist these bandwagons because they simply don't make economic sense, zealots often begin crusades and enlist the court system[22] to stall indefinitely some practical, logical solutions that would benefit everyone.

We each have responsibility to consider all facts available before subscribing to 'change' initiatives – and using our intelligence to evaluate issues rather than automatically deferring to convenient mass media viewpoints!

---

[21] See **Political Correctness**
[22] See **Justice System**

# Character

*"Character is doing the right thing when nobody's looking. There are too many people who think that the only thing that's right is to get by, and the only thing that's wrong is to get caught."*
*- J.C. Watts*

The best indication of one's character is his or her demonstration of ethics, honesty, courage and integrity. When selecting political leaders and business associates and in social relationships, character was once a priority for most of us. Why has this changed? Why are we now willing to overlook so much? Are one's principles not important?

If we are willing to downgrade our expectations of others – or even worse, our own personal standards - we are kidding ourselves that our society can maintain order and maintain its envied worldwide leadership position. We should select leaders, vendors and friends who demonstrate character of the highest degree. We all have character flaws - but honesty doesn't have 'degrees' – just like one can't be just a 'little bit pregnant'. Re-establish high expectations for yourself and others!

Refuse to compromise personal standards just because prominent leaders fail to demonstrate high standards. Elect only leaders who articulate principles and demonstrate the highest standards of character!

One's actions are the most accurate indications of one's character.

# Choices

*"Every choice you make has an end result."*
*- Zig Ziglar*

What can be more obvious?

Within our society are many individuals who refuse to see that their circumstance is the result their own decision-making [23], choosing instead to blame someone or something external. By providing individual 'bailouts', such as welfare, we reinforce these bad choices. Are we doing these individuals a favor by reinforcing this concept?[24]

Our welfare system, our legal system, our insurance system and even our government subtly promotes the idea that if one makes a bad decision, they can often be made 'whole' by the 'system'.[25]

Why are welfare payments not linked to clean drug tests and verified educational or employment-seeking efforts? Why do we allow frivolous lawsuits that exploit the flawed legal system[26] in achieving payouts in spite of innocence? Why do we bail out individuals, managers, municipalities and even states that continue to make poor decisions?

Our country needs to eliminate the entitlement vehicles that reward poor choices. Elect leaders that understand this and are willing to sell it to those that don't understand it!

---

[23] See **Rights vs. Responsibilities**
[24] See **Entitlement**
[25] See **Bailouts**
[26] See **Justice System**

# Closed Minds

*"The only way to entertain some folks is to listen to them."*
*- Kin Hubbard*

An old friend once advised not to try to '...pry open a closed mind...' Given the rate of change in our society, no mature individual can afford to be closed-minded about change. Resisting the inevitable is simply denial, and not an attitude compatible with productive living. Refusing to consider new ideas, new possibilities for our own careers or lifestyles will only earn one the label of closed-mindedness.

This is not to suggest that we should be flexible when it comes to defending our principles – the underlying values we believe are essential to ethical, moral living. Being closed-minded about the minimum expectations we have for others is part of having character and living a principled life!

Be sure to examine those who exhibit closed-mindedness about a given issue to determine if their position is due to a flawed belief system, a lack of information, or a matter of principle. Counsel them. Educate them. It can make a huge difference!

*"The mind of a bigot is like the pupil of the eye.*
*The more light you shine on it, the more it will contract."*
*-- Oliver Wendell Holmes Jr.*

# Common Sense

*"The laws of common sense do not change according to scale.
If it doesn't work in your own checkbook, it won't work in theirs.
If it doesn't work at your house, it won't work at the White House."*

*- Glenn Beck*

Common Sense is obviously not as 'common' as it should be.
Hardly a day goes by that we don't observe one of our leaders
saying or doing something downright stupid . . . and defending it
on some 'higher-intelligence' grounds.    Common Sense is a
'natural law'[27] that, again, no leader or ideologue can improve
upon or honestly (or intelligently) dispute.   Common Sense should
be one criterion for making all decisions, public and private.   Does
math work differently in congress than it does at home?   Are the
laws of physics suspended when they are not politically expedient?

The famous '*...they say...*' response often heard from folks
defending stupid opinions simply means that they heard someone
else say it!   Isn't it possible that your friend, your professor, your
boss or the media spokesperson could be wrong?

Union members strike when there is **no** hope of recovering the
wages lost during the strike in a new contract.   We perform full
body searches on 4 year-olds and 90 year-olds at airports when
both are incapable of causing a breach of security.   We ask
questions when we already know the answers!   Why do the same
things over and over and expect a different result?   Why investigate
something when we already know the facts and solution?

---

[27] See **Natural Laws**

It is particularly distressing when our leaders no longer practice or appreciate the principles of common sense. The 'over-analysis' of simple problems, the endless 'studies' and 'investigations' are examples of procrastination, decision-avoidance, and delays in assigning responsibility when the obvious, common sense solution is well known.

*"The charge is often made against the intelligentsia and other members of the anointed that their theories and the policies based on them lack common sense. But the very commonness of common sense makes it unlikely to have any appeal to the anointed. How can they be wiser and nobler than everyone else while agreeing with everyone else?"*
*-Thomas Sowell*

Re-*valuing* common sense should be at the top of our lists!

*"We have now sunk to such depth that the re-statement of the obvious has become the duty of all intelligent men."*
*-George Orwell*

*Common sense is not always a gift.*
*It can be a punishment because*
*you have to deal with everyone*
*who doesn't have it!*
*-unknown*

# Comparative Rationalization

*"Your ability to rationalize your own bad deeds
makes you believe that the whole world
is as amoral as you are"*
*- Douglas Coupland*

As children, we often heard, *'...Susie made me do it...'*
As teenagers, our excuse was often *'...everyone else is doing it...'*
Of course, neither of these excuses was acceptable nor logical by
mature adult standards! So why is it today, when questioned about
a lack of performance or lack of forthrightness, even leaders at the
very top are quick to ask that we look at their predecessors and
observe that *'they'* didn't solve the problem either . . . or that
*'they'* weren't totally honest either . . . or, worse yet, that *'they'*
possessed some totally unrelated flaw!

Making an excuse for your own poor behavior or lack of judgment
by comparing yourself with someone who may have performed
even more poorly is admitting that you have run out of original
thoughts and have no idea how to solve the problem under
discussion. It classifies you as incompetent. One can always find
a person of lower accomplishment to 'self-compare' with.
Obviously an intelligent, mature leader would discuss ideas,
alternatives and solutions - not make excuses!

Anyone using this tactic should be labeled as inept and labeled as
such, loudly and publically! Letters to the editor, emails to friends,
and persistent calls to the media would be a great beginning!

# Conservation

*"The waste of plenty is the resource of scarcity."*
*- Thomas Love Peacock*

One responsibility of active citizenship is the conservation of *all* resources, not just the non-renewable ones.[28] While this may sound like a 'green' issue - it extends far beyond that. While parts of our globe are virtually uninhabited, others are very densely populated. Sooner or later, the infinite availability of food, energy and other life-sustaining resources will become more difficult (and/or prohibitively expensive) to obtain. Intelligence, logic, and plain common sense dictate that conservation be a part of our daily thought process.

We have become such a throw-away society that we take for granted the unlimited availability of everything we need. Energy - whether gasoline or household electricity - not only costs money, but does absolutely no good for anyone if wasted. It is foolish and economically illiterate to waste lumber, food, and other commodities used daily! On a personal level time, for example, is a resource that is very finite - and if we waste time, we limit our own potential for accomplishment.

Just because we can 'afford' things is not just cause to waste. Saving time and unnecessary expense is just plain common sense - wasting is lazy and un-disciplined.

---

[28] See **Waste**

# Contrived Objectivity

*"We finally found out the real problem with the mainstream media: They're agnostic on sanity."*
*- Arianna Huffington*

We've seen it and heard it over and over again . . . phrases like 'we tell it like it is', 'we report, you decide', 'get the real story', 'the spin-free zone', and 'all the news that's fit to print'. In the name of objectivity, the media[29] pretends that they are neutral (but expert) on every issue when virtually every minute of air time and almost every column-inch is full of opinion, shallow analysis and, typically, the application of sensationalism.

We should also look with jaundiced eye at those who boldly and proudly fetishize the arrogance of elected officials when they speak from their bully pulpits with self-declared authority on almost every subject. The climax comes when the media 'objectively' features those who declare that they '...know better than their constituents what is best for the country...'[30]

Mass media programming, usually in talk-show formats but labeled as 'investigative reporting', tries court cases, convicts suspects, and declares whether justice will be served without anything more than a few 'experts' conversing[31] about and analyzing the 'news' reports of other media reporters!

Applying even the most elementary level of common sense should allow each of us to form responses that reflect better intelligence.

---

[29] See **Media**
[30] See **Bureaucrats**
[31] See **'I Think'**

# Corruption

*"Power tends to corrupt,*
*and absolute power corrupts absolutely...."*
*- Lord Acton*

It should be obvious that the dishonest "...abuse of public power for private gain..." is both criminal and destructive. It is not a matter of 'degree' or justified by the common statement that 'everyone does it'.[32] Carried to the extreme degree, we have all observed what third-world leaders accomplish when hoarding the public wealth for private purposes while starving their countrymen.

Sadly, there are many whose primary (or only) motivation for honesty is the fear of getting 'caught'. This defines their character.[33] It indicates that honesty is a foreign concept to them. (If it is not a foreign concept, it at least has 'relative' levels of applicability) It should indicate to the rest of us that these individuals are not leadership material.

Restoring faith in our leadership will require a massive paradigm shift - from those that see public office as a way of creating personal wealth and notoriety at all costs, to honest individuals who genuinely understand the definition of accountability, understand the tasks at hand, and are truly committed to performing 'public service'. Such individuals take pride in solving problems and gaining the respect of the masses – nothing else!

---

[32] See **Comparative Rationalization, Cronyism**
[33] See **Character**

# Courage

*"We must have courage to bet on our ideas, to take the calculated risk, and to act. Everyday living requires courage if life is to be effective and bring happiness."*
*- Maxwell Maltz*

Exhibiting courage is becoming less and less popular. Courage often involves 'doing-something-different' or promoting change. The push-back when advocating change [34] is tremendous and immediate today, due in part to the electronic age and social media channels. It is human nature to avoid pain – and demonstrating courage can be intimidating.

It should be obvious, however, that most significant developments in history were initiated by individuals who courageously 'stuck their necks out' and advocated change of some sort.

Personal displays of courage – in taking risks or demonstrating bravery are, however, respected by peers and often rewarded – if not monetarily, at least in in self-satisfaction.

Entrepreneurship is another act of courage that reveals a commitment to productivity, accountability and capitalism – qualities that today are undervalued but extremely important.

*"The test of courage comes when we are in the minority. The test of tolerance comes when we are in the majority."*
*-- Ralph W. Sockman*

---

[34] See **Change**

# Crisis in Confidence

*"If once you forfeit the confidence of your fellow-citizens, you can never regain their respect and esteem."*
*-Abraham Lincoln*

Many Americans are rapidly losing confidence in our governance and very close to believing that our economic system may never return to historically efficient and productive levels.

When corporate scandals fail to generate swift rebuke; when political corruption is shrugged away as routine; and wars are fought with non-specific strategies, intelligent citizens must rally behind principle and take action. Without proactive initiatives, the decay in confidence will continue.

True leaders constantly re-evaluate current issues; speak definitively as to their priorities, change their positions when appropriate and assume new risks. Admittedly, this kind of leader may be labeled as a radical, an extremist, or even a dissident – but drastic measures are usually needed to meet harsh challenges!

Topics for this discussion include governmental reorganization consistent with the constitution, a practical and comprehensive national energy policy, limits on lobbyists, a code of ethics for public office-holders, an economic strategy constructed by experts rather than politicians, and defined criteria for foreign aid and military involvement. It's been said that you can move forward or backward – but you can never stand still.

Only strong leadership[35] will confront this declining confidence.

---

[35] See **Leadership**

# Creativity

*"Creativity is a great motivator because it
makes people interested in what they are doing.
Creativity gives hope that there can be a worthwhile idea.
Creativity gives the possibility of some sort of achievement to everyone.
Creativity makes life more fun and more interesting."*
*- Edward de Bono*

Originality is an interesting word – and more interestingly applied our personal tasks, our relationships, and businesses activities. It is defined as '...the use of imagination or original ideas...' – and popularly referred to as out-of-the-box-thinking, resourcefulness, ingenuity, and originality.

Without a doubt, some of the people you remember the most are those who surprise you with ideas, suggest solutions that you would have never thought of, or involve themselves in unusual activities.

The *value* in being creative is that you distinguish yourself from others, making yourself more valuable to employers, more attractive in personal relationships and very likely happier in your personal pursuits.

Combined with entrepreneurship[36], the sky is the limit in your personal growth and accumulation of wealth.

---

[36] See **Entrepreneurship**

# Criticism

*"Honest criticism is hard to take - especially when it comes from a relative, a friend, an acquaintance, or a stranger."*
*- Franklin P. Jones*

Criticism comes in many forms . . . but the important issue is how criticism is received and one's response to it. Any creative or courageous activity is likely to be observed by others and a reaction generated. Depending on their motivation, intelligence and opportunity, you may receive criticism.

Whether selfishly motivated, intelligently constructed, or purely emotional, one should be thankful for all criticism. It is the basis for thoroughly scrutinizing and evaluating your own activities. It may introduce a flaw in your process that needs addressing. It may simply awaken you to the challenges in 'selling'[37] your ideas.

If you receive no criticism, your activity or idea may be so bland as to be worthless . . .

*"If you are not criticized, you may not be doing much."*
*- Donald H. Rumsfeld*

---

[37] See **Salesmanship**

# Cronyism

*"The big debate between the two factions in Washington boils down to nothing more than a contest over power and political cronyism, rather than any deep philosophic differences."*

—Ron Paul

There are two important and harmful dimensions to the cronyism present in business and government. One is the decrease in performance, efficiency and practical progress that occurs when the best person or best company is not selected to do a job. The second is the borderline or downright criminal nature of doing something for the wrong reasons and/or by unethical means.

Appointing non-qualified persons to jobs that involve important problem-solving, quite frankly, should be classified as 'criminal' even when not illegal. The same criteria[38] used for selecting public leaders should be applied to all appointments and hiring.

Attaching unrelated earmarks to bills in Congress is essentially the same thing – rewarding friends, lobbyists, or constituents for the wrong reasons and by underhanded, almost-secretive means. Again, our society cannot afford to continue this practice.

If true qualified leaders are in charge, and open and transparent practices followed, cronyism would be minimized. Earmarks should be eliminated immediately and completely. Unethical practices in the selection of vendors should be prosecuted and participants penalized.

---

[38] See **Bureaucrats**

# Culture

*'...the set of shared attitudes, values, goals, and practices that characterizes an institution or organization...'*

*-Merriam-Webster*

One issue that continuously clouds our practices in international diplomacy and foreign relations is the ignorance of 'cultural' differences. Further, when our own leaders attempt to shape and manipulate the historical 'culture' of our own citizenry, confusion reigns with deepening dysfunctionality.

Wikipedia describes 'culture' as the '...arts and other manifestations of human intellectual achievement regarded collectively...'. Individual and collective values[39] and beliefs of the masses can never be ignored in forming strategies or defining relationships. Expecting foreign governments to react rationally implies that they think and believe the same way we do. Expecting our own citizens to accept a radical proposition is to ignore traditions, beliefs, and emotions. Expecting laws to erase prejudices is unrealistic. Providing incentives to change without corresponding penalties for failure to change has

Respect for and the acknowledgement of deep-seated cultural mores is the first step toward successful relationships. Observation of historical practices is the only indicator of future practices. Throwing money at problems only fortifies the status quo. The government should not attempt to shape culture: the money spent on public radio, the arts, et al., is an affront to the Constitution.

---

[39] See **Values**

# Demagogue

*...a political leader who seeks support by appealing to popular desires and prejudices rather than by using rational argument...*

Today's political environment is so polluted with demagogues that this topic hardly needs dialogue. Intelligent citizens should be outraged and insulted by the rhetoric [40], grandiosity [41], and posturing[42] coming from our news media, politicians and leaders. Even worse, the time and resources consumed in delivering this manipulative and misleading dialogue totally replaces the effort that should be spent on critical issues that need diligent attention.

Our 'reactionary' press and politicians need to be reminded that, while they are setting their agendas based on the emotional outcry of the hour, known critical issues with monumental consequences are looming in the background with no solutions being discussed. Urgent but non-important issues get on the agenda while very important but non-urgent issues get no attention. Telling audiences what they 'want' to hear instead of what they 'need' to hear may be popular – but it should be suicidal.

As impossible as it may be, re-establishing priorities should be the focus of all of our leaders – and we, as citizens, should insist on it. No business survives very long if it ignores long-range planning in favor of putting out short term 'fires'. No business leader survives if he or she continuously fails to 'level' with stakeholders.

---

[40] See **Rhetoric**
[41] See **Grandiosity**
[42] See **Posturing**

# Demonstrations

*"In civilized societies, if you are offended by a cartoon, you do not burn flags, take up guns and raid buildings, chant death to your opponents, or threaten suicide bombings. You write a letter to the editor."*

*-Michelle Malkin*

Demonstrators, with few exceptions, represent the entitlement class. The practice of demonstrating has evolved as a manifestation of 'free speech' among people with no real power over their lives who are void of any intelligent analysis or creativity in their strategy. This mob mentality rarely produces meaningful change.

The speeches heard during demonstrations are often absent of rational thought and full of the rhetoric and misleading statements – usually designed more to incite emotions than solve problems. The press coverage of these events, or lack thereof, gives more or less credibility to the causes and directs public opinion on a purely emotional level. This, by itself, is damaging because it gives undeserved credibility to the unintelligent, unproductive and/or unrealistic ideas often adopted by those who refuse to think for themselves.

A civilized, intelligent, and more effective way to induce change is to behave like a lobbyist. Lobbyists 'sell' [43] their ideas to legislators who can introduce change. In spite of their negative attributes, lobbyists do their homework, determine a plausible plan, and approach those who have the power to do something about it. Demonstrators do none of the above.

---

[43] See **Salesmanship**

# Denial

*"Hope is the denial of reality."*
*- Margaret Weis*

Denial is refusing to acknowledge the existence or seriousness of unpleasant realities. We can call it human nature - the avoidance of things we don't like . . . but when we observe denial in our leaders, it's time for a change. It's a sign of immaturity, of weakness, and the absence of appropriate leadership skills.

In politics we often call it '...kicking the can down the road...', a technique that avoids solving the problem and attempts to place responsibility and potential blame on future office holders. On a personal level, it allows professional counselors to rack up billable hours while they help individuals 'deal' with their denial. Any delay in dealing with an unpleasant reality is counterproductive at the least, and expensive and wasteful at the worst. It is also dishonest when done consciously and deliberately at the expense of constituents.

Eliminating this phenomenon requires that we pick and choose leaders carefully. Listen to them identify issues and propose solutions. Do they acknowledge the problems you identify? Are they committed to implementing swift and effective solutions? Do they have a track record of keeping promises?[44]

*"Delay is the deadliest form of denial."*
*- C. Northcote Parkinson*

---

[44] See **Promises**

# Distractions

*"America is addicted to wars of distraction"*
*- Barbara Ehrenreich*

Distractions come in two flavors.

A simple distraction is one that causes our focus[45] to be realigned. We allow friends, environmental events or the media to interrupt our current activities – causing us to redirect our thought processes and our physical undertakings. The net effect is that we expend energy on non-priority items, become less productive, and fail to meet our own expectations and objectives. Leadership abilities are often measured by one's ability to control and/or deal with distractions.

The second type of distraction is intentional. When faced with unpleasant topics or questions, many folks simply change the subject. Examples include answering a question with a question or throwing out an unrelated comparison that minimizes the issue under discussion.[46] Political candidates master this process – by speaking to their own agenda while ignoring specific questions. Such avoidance sidesteps the question – usually revealing one's unwillingness to face difficult issues.

Recognize distractions for what they are – and insist on promoting a productive agenda that is the result of your own thought, study and analysis!

---

[45] See **Focus**
[46] See **Comparative Rationalization**

# Dissatisfaction

*"If there is dissatisfaction with the status quo, good.*
*If there is ferment, so much the better.*
*If there is restlessness, I am pleased.*
*Then let there be ideas, and hard thought, and hard work.*
*If man feels small, let man make himself bigger."*
*- Hubert H. Humphrey*

The changes in governance necessary in our society will happen when the constituency becomes sufficiently dissatisfied! I would suggest that the level of dissatisfaction necessary for radical change is fast approaching!

Those who look forward are normally the first to recognize the need for substantive change – while those who live day-to-day are often late subscribers to the need for change. The bad news is that this timing gap is often strategically important in that the latter group may vote into power a leadership team that does not sufficiently identify with the first group!

Because changes caused by technology and market forces are happening so rapidly, we are constantly forced to play catch-up in our attempts to legislate changes in governance. The classic 'tail-wagging-the-dog' scenario comes to mind!

This is solved by selecting leaders that are intelligent, mature and who act creatively and proactively. Such leaders become dissatisfied by a lack of planning, apply common sense, and don't wait until a problem surfaces to become dissatisfied!

# Diversity (mandated)

*"It is as impossible to withhold education from the receptive mind, as it is impossible to force it upon the unreasoning."*
*- Agnes Repplier*

The existence of diversity in business and society should be recognized for the learning opportunities and educational benefits that result. The recognition of cultural diversity and the creative productivity that can result is to be celebrated. However, the practice of forced quotas, endless politically-correct mandates, timetables and penalties are best described as misdirected energy.

At worst, it is foolish and wasteful.

Rewarding individuals based on ethnicity rather than their talents and/or performance is wrong.[47] *Forcing* individuals to change attitudes and viewpoints has never worked - educating them has a fighting chance for positive change. Resources would be far better applied toward educating folks in the virtues of ethics, proper decision-making, respect, honesty, fairness and appropriate behaviors.

Forcing artificial relationships in contrived environments and expending time and money to force 'diversity' in the workplace simply reduces efficiency, creates subtle prejudices and prevents reasonable folks from making common sense decisions.

---

[47] See **Affirmative Action**

# <u>Do</u> Something Different!

*"There is nothing so useless as doing efficiently
that which should not be done at all."*
*- Peter Drucker*

A similarly relevant quote goes something like '…it's strange how we continue to do the same thing over and over and expect a different result…' Being in denial [48] about obvious issues condemns us to a future of disappointment and deterioration. Our human nature wants to shy away from unpleasant things while pursuing pleasurable things – but maturity dictates that we prioritize and deal with all of the issues in front of us.

Just as true leaders[49] are measured by their accomplishments and the respect afforded them by their followers, individuals can impact their circumstances by changing habits and engaging in behaviors that lead to success. Being silent or speaking 'to the choir' will not replace diligent action.

We all need to embrace the idea that changing[50] our day-to-day activities can and will lead to better results – for ourselves and our society. Make some time in each day to communicate with those that can make new things happen!

*"It is a common delusion that you make
things better by talking about them."*
*- Dame Rose Macaulay*

---

[48] See **Denial**
[49] See **Leadership**
[50] See **Change**

# Drama Queens

A Drama Queen is someone who builds something unimportant into a major issue. A Drama Queen is someone who routinely blows things out of proportion. Drama Queens seem to have an emotional dysfunction that requires that they draw those around them into their over-reactional state of mind.

We all know individuals that possess this characteristic . . . and we can choose to avoid them, ignore their behavior, or reinforce it. It's very important that we not respond with 'I understand!'[51]

It is very difficult to ignore the ultimate Drama Queens - the media outlets,[52] particularly the television networks, in our country. While they claim to 'report' the news, they have transitioned into powerful influence machines that exert considerable control over the outcomes of elections, significantly impact economic trends, and influence personal attitudes toward a variety of issues. Unfortunately, the 'drama queen' factor dominates their style and content! Why are days of coverage devoted to one mentally deranged individual on trial while only minutes are devoted to major national issues? Common sense doesn't support speculating about 'anticipated' minor events while ignoring 'real' major issues.

The goal of sensational reporting is to increase or sustain viewership or readership. This leads to a reduced focus on objective journalism in favor of profits while contributing to a distorted sense of priorities among viewers. Be very careful in listening to what is represented as 'journalism' and 'news'.

---

[51] See **I Understand**
[52] See **Media**

# Dysfunctional

Truly dysfunctional folks are **unable** to look at a situation, make a rational observation, and react appropriately utilizing common sense. Dysfunctional adult behaviors are learned primarily by imitating role models, whether family or friends. As a result, those who are dysfunctional may, many times, propagate more dysfunctionality among their families and friends.

Anyone who lacks common sense is automatically somewhat dysfunctional. Of course we're talking in degrees - and we normally reserve the 'dysfunctional' label for those who are unable to cope with daily situations and issues in a socially acceptable way. However, this label should be applied to individuals as well as organizations that don't perform to accepted standards.

We should all refuse to accept the behaviors of those that promote chaos or respond illogically. Immature, illogical, and/or dysfunctional behavior is reinforced by passive non-reactions on the part of highly functional adults.

The obvious solution is to proactively point out dysfunctional responses. Merely saying 'I understand'[53] to those who respond irrationally or illogically is usually taken as your approval of their responses and actions. Don't do it! At least say, 'I hear what you are saying but do not agree . . . or "What you are saying (or doing) doesn't make any sense!"

---

[53] See 'I Understand'

# Earmarks

*"The earmark favor factory needs to be boarded up and demolished, not turned over to new management that may or may not have a better eye for earmarks with 'merit.' "*

*- Tom Coburn*

Earmarks are synonymous with "pork barrel" legislation. Pork barrel politics refers to governmental spending that benefits the constituents of a given politician in return for their political support, either in the form of campaign contributions, influence, or votes.

When an elected legislator loudly proclaims that there are 'no earmarks' in a given piece of legislation, look closely - it is almost certainly full of them! Such actions are fraudulent, dishonest and wrong[54]. It is the exact definition of bribery - and most of us would go to jail for such an act! We should all campaign to completely eliminate earmarks and unrelated legislative amendments as part of the bill-passing process.

When these behaviors reach the highest offices in our land, it is time for a true uprising - a citizen's revolt against dishonesty and corruption. When our leaders are faced with clear expectations of honesty, and are impeached for breaching trust, things will change!

---

[54] See **Corruption**

# Education

*"It is a thousand times better to have common sense without education than to have education without common sense."*
*- Robert G. Ingersoll*

There is much that can be said about education - and where common sense fits into the educational process. We've seen highly 'educated' folks with absolutely no common sense[55] - and we've seen very wise folks with a great deal of common sense but little formal education. However, as Ingersoll says, common sense should be valued most highly!

The advantages of a liberal arts education as opposed to specialty concentrations have been discussed for many years. Exactly what makes this true is, in part, based on the concept that the higher education *experience* may have more to do with equipping a student for a career than specific subject matter knowledge. This suggests the development of practical common sense!

Let's not make it any more complicated than it is. As described in the chapter on intelligent incoherence, possessing significant knowledge without the ability to practically apply it leads to failure. Anyone who makes incoherent statements, uses flawed reasoning, or misuses facts to promote impractical or unworkable solutions may be educated - but lacking in common sense. We need both in our leaders . . . and in our personal relationships!

*"An education isn't how much you have committed to memory, or even how much you know. It's being able to differentiate between what you do know and what you don't."*
*- Anatole France*

---

[55] See **Intellectual Incoherence**

# Efficiency

Let's expand - there can only be economic growth where there is efficiency, therefore productivity, **greater** than that of our competitors. Our country and our culture will not survive if we are complacent and do not constantly pursue efficiency, economy and productivity in everything we do.

The laws of supply and demand and the free enterprise system are the 'natural' ways of guaranteeing efficiency, economy and productivity. If and when one supplier works harder to produce goods or services more efficiently than another, he is rewarded financially! It is also important to realize that we are competing in a global marketplace – it is not sufficient to compare our productivity with domestic competitors only.

An entire book should be written on the importance of exercising creativity in the pursuit of efficiency, economy and productivity in our daily lives - both on an individual level and in our work lives. Those who relax will remain in the lower economic strata while those who constantly strive for increased efficiency, economy and productivity will elevate their economic condition! Remember, the definition of wealth is where small efforts have big results . . . the definition of poverty is where big efforts have small results!

# Emotional Decisions

*"When dealing with people, remember you are not dealing with creatures of logic, but creatures of emotion."*
*- Dale Carnegie*

Decision-making is the process of choosing between alternatives. We all make hundreds of decisions every day. Sometimes we use logic to make decisions, using only a rational analysis of the alternatives. Sometimes we use our emotions, choosing what seems right (based on our belief system), the least painful, or the most satisfying. Common sense is the label applied to combining the facts we can obtain and the knowledge and experience we possess, with prudent, sound judgment.

Unfortunately, we often make totally emotional decisions. It is sometimes in 'reaction' to a particularly stressful moment. At times it is due to ulterior personal motives - like revenge. All too often, it is because we aren't disciplined. We don't care to (or take the time to) consider the facts, or analyze the alternatives and the consequences. Emotions, in these cases, override logic and even create false logic patterns represented to be factual.

Effective leaders cannot afford to make emotional decisions. They cannot yield to passionate, specious pleas by lobbyists. They must insulate themselves from those who present emotional, rather than factual, arguments.

Citizens who do not minimize their emotional reactions to candidates should not vote. Leaders who cannot defend their positions using common sense, historical data, and facts should not be in office.

# Entrepreneurship

*"Entrepreneurship drives innovation.*
*Innovation drives productivity.*
*Productivity drives higher wages and higher standards of living."*
*- Sandy K. Baruah*

The history of success of our western society is undeniably rooted in entrepreneurship. Without the risk-takers that started businesses based on having an idea, a better idea or a radically new idea, progress would simply not have occurred. Today entrepreneurship takes place on multiple levels. Not all entrepreneurial individuals - are sole proprietors in start-up businesses. They may be found in large businesses and 'occasionally' in government.

The relevant characteristics essential to growth and success are discussed in the chapters on budgeting, supply and demand, the free enterprise system and almost every chapter in this book. However, one important concept, fully understood by all entrepreneurs, is the necessity of generating profits . . . because the failure to maintain profitability means losing one's enterprise, and consequently, one's personal investment.

Rewarding entrepreneurial attitudes and qualities within any organization is essential to motivating staff, assuring financial profitability and enhancing sustainability because new ideas are essential to growth. Entrepreneurs within large businesses or the government will be most successful if they treat the enterprise as if it were their own.

Judge those in leadership positions by how they embrace and practice entrepreneurial principles!

# Energy & Oil

There is no energy shortage. The United States has incredibly sufficient oil reserves. The primary problem is governmental restrictions that tie the hands of domestic energy producers resulting in foreign dependence. We've debated the solutions to the 'energy crises' at all levels. From the individual household level to the public utility level, no one has offered a credible master plan for achieving fossil fuel independence. When we throw in 'green' initiatives and the political climate, there is no short-term hope for significant alternatives reducing fossil fuel consumption.

Aside from more properly labeling our efforts as 'conservation',[56] it would seem that one mutually agreed-upon objective is to reduce our dependence on *foreign* oil. The *only* workable solution is allowing the 'natural laws' of supply and demand and the free enterprise system to work. It's far simpler than we're making it!

Instead of taxing those that consume, let's pass legislation that requires the domestic refiners of automotive fuel to use a maximum of 90% foreign crude oil next year – ramping down 10% each year to a maximum of 10% foreign oil 10 years from now. Couple this with the removal of all domestic drilling restrictions (of course requiring that oil companies clean up any mess they create) and the 'natural laws' will take care of the rest. Auto manufacturers will develop more efficient cars and consumers will buy cars they can afford to operate, as fuel prices may rise.

It's not *that* complex!

---

[56] See **Green**

# Entitlement

By definition, entitlement is a guarantee of a benefit based on governmental policy or legislation. It is the notion that one deserves a reward or benefit without any obligation, investment or effort on his or her part. Often used as a synonym is the concept of rights[57] - which is an entitlement, but based on a moral or social principle. Entitlements, as they exist today, have grown far beyond sensible levels or these definitions.

When someone screams, 'I know my rights!' or 'I have a right to _____', you can bet they are expecting something for nothing or are evading personal responsibility. The social problem created by this mentality is that one can do less and, by manipulating the system, receive more!

The 'unalienable rights' guaranteed by the constitution (Life, Liberty and the pursuit of Happiness) is right on the mark – we each have our life and liberty – and the *'right'* to pursue happiness. To believe that happiness should be handed to us is absurd.

No one is entitled to something for nothing – and certainly not to a reward for making bad decisions. It's time for tough love – and the application of reality to those with an entitlement mentality.

---

[57] See **Rights vs. Responsibilities**

# Ethics

*"Ethics is knowing the difference between what you have a right to do and what is right to do."*
*- Potter Stewart*

Again, a simple word whose definition has been convoluted beyond belief! Ethics is the '...social, religious, and civil code of conduct' considered to be correct and appropriate to maintaining our culture. It is the definition of the moral values of human behavior that govern a rational culture. It is defining good vs. evil, right vs. wrong, and virtue vs. vice.

Our society will never hold (or regain) a position of preeminence if ethical behavior is not present in ALL leadership, in all governing bodies, and in all personal decision-making.

Conditional ethics, or the belief that the rules change based on the circumstances, is not true ethics but the failure or absence of the application of ethics.[58]

An official code of conduct exists in most of our governing bodies and corporate entities. Perhaps plastering it in visible places would remind everyone of the principles they are obligated to follow.

Common sense dictates that existing rules and laws should be enforced until officially modified! Those who suggest otherwise are not upholding their oath of office! Infractions should be followed by swift and efficient recall, impeachment, firings or the like!

---

[58] See **Corruption, Cronyism, & Earmarks**

# Exceptionalism

*"America's greatness, America's exceptional greatness, is not based on that fact that we are the most powerful, most prosperous – and most generous – nation anywhere on earth. Rather, those things are the result of American Exceptionalism."*

*- Newt Gingerich*

Recognition of the fact that a person, country, society, or institution, is "exceptional" in some way should certainly not be controversial - nor should it be considered to be a negative characteristic! That our nation has the ability to help others and aid in crises is to be celebrated! That we have the ability *and* *choose* to be generous speaks to our collective character.

However, believing that this characteristic entitles us to avoid responsibility or behave in a way not conforming to good principles is absurd. The application of ethics, responsible behavior and common sense decisions must follow in order to maintain our exceptionalism.

Tradition, timidity, denial, the bureaucratic process and corruption are seriously threatening our exceptionalism today. Without a return to ethical practices, zero-based budgeting and efficient government, our exceptionalism will very soon disappear.

# Expectations

*"Was there ever a bigger case of liberal whining, persecution complex, myopia, narcissism, and inflated sense of entitlement."*

*- James Delingpole*

As an adjunct to the subject of 'entitlement'[59], the expectations and beliefs of the average citizen need to be discussed and labeled. I should refrain from using the word 'average' because there are two different groups that we should identify, both of which cannot be considered as 'average' at the same time. Each group may be considered 'normal' or dominate the other from time to time by virtue of size, influence and position within government and society, but they have vastly different characteristics.

First are those who expect their government to provide an infrastructure that provides basic domestic safety, protection from foreign threats and essential services like courtrooms, highways and utilities. They expect to work for a living, live within their means and take responsibility for their decisions and actions.

The second group expects virtually everything they cannot easily obtain on their own to be handed to them in the form of subsidies, handouts, bailouts or other programs. They demand their 'rights'[60] on a regular basis and always seem to have time to 'demonstrate'.[61]

It should be clear which group built our country, represents the values of our culture, sustains our economy and should make governing decisions.

---

[59] See **Entitlement**
[60] See **Rights vs. Responsibilities**
[61] See **Demonstrations**

# Experience

*"Human beings, who are almost unique in having the ability to learn from the experience of others, are also remarkable for their apparent disinclination to do so."*
*- Douglas Adams*

A great deal has been written about experience – how some learn from personal experiences, and some from the experiences of others, and how some ignore all of the lessons, over and over.

An intelligent individual learns from personal experiences; observation, (the experiences of others); and the practical application of their own analysis (often involving the rejection of common opinions).

However, it takes courage to reject tradition and popular beliefs. This book is an attempt to persuade more folks to question, to make personal observations, and to analyze for themselves – rather than accept the common (often media-delivered) perspective on daily issues. It is often sufficient to apply common sense – that innate, God-given internal ability to observe, analyze and react with – '..that makes sense…' or '…that doesn't make sense!...'

As one once said, there are leaders; there are followers, and there are those who don't know how to get out of the way.

# Facts vs. Opinions

*"You are entitled to your opinion.*
*But you are not entitled to your own facts."*
*- Daniel Patrick Moynihan*

In modern debate, especially where the mass media is involved, facts and opinions are rarely separated. Many choose to believe[62] that, if delivered via television, it must be factual – particularly when it is what *they want to believe*. One newscaster takes another newscaster's statement (which may have come from another newscaster's statement) and builds a case that rivals a supreme court argument – when little or no factual basis exists. Popular opinion then mushrooms and little chance for the truth exists. Nationwide demonstrations are organized by individuals that react emotionally to an opinion disguised as factual.

It is time that the all-powerful media begins acting responsibly and separating facts from opinions in a very deliberate way. The competition for ratings must somehow be redirected to be a contest for accuracy. This will happen only if viewers recognize what they are being fed and reject the manipulation. In the end, the common sense test must be applied.

*"People don't ask for facts in making up their minds. They would rather have one good, soul-satisfying emotion than a dozen facts."*
*- Robert Keith Leavitt*

*"I'm not sure I want popular opinion on my side -- I've noticed those with the most opinions often have the fewest facts."*
*- Bethania McKenstry*

---

[62] See **Beliefs**

# Fairness

*"Life is not fair; get used to it."*
*- Bill Gates*

'It's not fair!' is an expression often heard from children, from parties in a legal dispute and from idealists in all walks of life. We have inevitably been raised (or taught) to believe that life should be fair and that when it isn't, someone should step in, correct the situation, and cause it to become fair!

Unfortunately, as Bill Gates once told a group of students, life is not always fair. People are not always rational, customers are not always right, and parents do not always know best. Rules change, people will disappoint, and things one could *always* count on may fail tomorrow!

Very simply, dealing with such situations is a matter of choosing from the alternatives available – not declaring 'foul' or complaining. Alternatives include accepting the situation, working to cause change, or proposing an intelligent compromise. Mature individuals understand this.

The bad news is that a significant number of otherwise-intelligent adults do not understand this – choosing instead to demonstrate[63], participate in gridlock[64], or scream about their 'rights'[65]. These folks do not belong in positions of responsibility, leadership or government.

The follow-on to the quote above is, '…but make the most of it!'

---

[63] See **Demonstrations**
[64] See **Gridlock**
[65] See **Rights and Responsibilities**

# Federal Agencies

It is essential for a government to function that a certain number of 'agencies' or departments exist to monitor, regulate, and/or enforce policies and laws. Clear goals and limitations should be established at the onset that very specifically define an agency's mission. Problems begin when these agencies overstep practical boundaries, operate inefficiently or abandon common sense in executing their responsibilities. Clearly, governmental agencies need to be reminded daily that they exist solely to serve the public and enhance the quality of life of citizens, not to build empires under their own banners.

In order for an 'agency' to be respected, functional and justify its existence, it must be run like a 'business' with a management team that thinks more like an entrepreneur than a political appointee. Until this happens, our governmental agencies will never run efficiently, be respected or gain the full cooperation of constituents. As impossible as this seems, removing cronyism[66] and the resulting corruption should be our goal.

Making every agency compete with private enterprise for operating contracts is one way to assure efficiency. Incentive pay for performance should replace bloated salaries based on historical practices. Unions should be outlawed in public entities and conflict of interest employment relationship scenarios strictly enforced.

---

[66] See **Cronyism**

# Feelings

*"I've learned that people will forget what you said, people will forget what you did, but people will never forget how you made them feel."*
*-Maya Angelou*

Obviously this subject can take a number of directions – but for the sake of reinforcing the concept of simplifying complex issues, we will focus on the role of feelings in voting and other critical decision making.

One huge issue is the belief system(s) [67] we've individually developed during our lives. Beliefs, often synonymous with feelings, tend to mask facts [68] and distort one's ability to make rational decisions. Resistance to change [69] is another huge factor that reinforces 'feelings' and often delays appropriate decision making and actions.

Because we are human beings, feelings will never be absent from our thought processes and decision making. Just be careful to allow rationality to overrule feelings when faced with important life-altering decisions!

---

[67] See **Belief Systems**
[68] See **Facts vs. Opinions**
[69] See **Change**

# Fiscal Policy

*"I could end the deficit in 5 minutes; You just pass a law that says that anytime there is a deficit of more than 3% of GDP, all sitting members of Congress are ineligible for re-election."*
*-Warren Buffet*

As in budgeting[70], it is a monumental travesty that our elected leaders believe that spending 40% more than they 'take in' year after year is smart, logical, justifiable, sustainable or mandatory.

It reflects on their intelligence, demonstrates their priorities, brings into question their honesty, and suggests that their constituency is asleep.

We all know how a checkbook works. . . and as someone very wise once said, 'if it won't work in your house, it won't work in the White House!'[71]

In small business borrowings, banks require that owners sign personal guarantees when the repayment plan is not absolutely assured from multiple sources. If we suggested that our legislators 'sign personally' for borrowings, the excess-borrowing problem would be resolved very quickly!

We must all insist that a balanced budget be an immediate and mandatory priority.

---

[70] See **Budgets**
[71] See **Common Sense**

# Free Enterprise System

*"The inherent vice of capitalism is the unequal sharing of blessings;
the inherent virtue of socialism is the equal sharing of miseries"*
*- Winston Churchill*

The ability to practice entrepreneurship[72] in our country is the single, most powerful factor behind our economic prosperity. No governmental entity or regulated industry operates as efficiently or as responsively to consumer needs and economic demand as a purely entrepreneurial business governed by the law of supply and demand[73] in our free enterprise system.

The implications are far-reaching. Allowing capitalism and the principles of free enterprise[74] to exist reduces the need for large government; enhances the lifestyles of those that contribute and 'earn' their way; and is very self-regulating in the long term. Have you ever wondered why third world and formerly communist countries begin thriving as soon as entrepreneurship and free enterprise principles are implemented? Is it a mystery that immigrants flock to our country, in large, because of this opportunity?

Those that believe there to be better systems should review history and make a case for an alternative. It can't be done.

*"Underlying most arguments against the free market
is a lack of belief in freedom itself."*
*- Milton Friedman*

---

[72] See **Entrepreneurship**
[73] See **Supply and Demand**
[74] See **Private Enterprise**

# Freedom of Speech

*"People demand freedom of speech as a compensation for the freedom of thought which they seldom use."*
*-- Soren Kierkegaard*

The concept of freedom of speech has become a battle cry for many who confuse rationality with the perceived 'right' to be immature and stupid.

Delivering a speech full of emotion and selective 'facts' is one way to get heads nodding and those who *want* to believe, believing! Unfortunately, the responsibility that accompanies mature speechmaking is all too often ignored – and audiences fail to discount such speechmakers.

Free speech is a powerful component of democracy and, while no one should advocate for restrictions, intelligent audiences must demonstrate their ability to ignore irresponsible speechmaking and call-out leaders who deliver specious arguments and confuse facts with opinions.[75]

*"Facts do not cease to exist because they are ignored."*
*- Aldous Huxley*

---

[75] See **Facts vs. Opinions**

# Focus

*"One reason so few of us achieve what we truly want is that we never direct our focus; we never concentrate our power. Most people dabble their way through life, never deciding to master anything in particular."*
*- Tony Robbins*

Personal habits have always been very difficult to change.[76] Personal accomplishments, as a result, suffer as compared to one's potential. Procrastination, indecisiveness, emotional issues, distractions, a lack of resources and many other factors often inject interruptions into our daily routines compromising our 'focus' on important things.

Success stories all seem to have one element in common – the protagonist had a goal and a commitment to achieving that goal. If one characteristic is common to the failure of our country's policies today, it is that our leadership cannot prioritize the issues before us and focus on any one of them until solved.[77] Admittedly the challenges are great – but true leaders prioritize[78] issues, establish goals, organize resources, delegate tasks, and implement solutions on a timetable. It's **NOT** That Complex!

---

[76] See **Change**
[77] See **Gridlock**
[78] See **Priorities**

# 'Follow the Money'

While the origin of the phrase is often attributed to the book and movie 'All the President's Men', the concept that 'following the money' will lead to the source of the issue is much older.

Conceptually, greed and the pursuit of monetary gain will always lay out a traceable course to follow when a mystery exists as to who or what is behind a given development. Decisions that don't make immediate sense, or results that seem to defy logic often lead to head-scratching and raised eyebrows.

In the political arena particularly, 'deals' that don't make sense often make all the sense in the world to *someone's* pocketbook. When one's wealth grows exponentially without any visible cause, 'following the money' will often lead to an explanation that borders on being ethical.[79]

Explanations that rhyme with 'too good to be true' are often not.

---

[79] See **Ethics**

# Foreign Aid

*"....government-to-government 'foreign aid' . . . is a transfer from the poor in rich countries to the rich in poor countries."*
*- Peter Bauer*

Common sense needs to be injected into the foreign aid policies and practices of our government. It doesn't take a rocket scientist to observe that a great deal of our foreign aid simply contributes to the corruption of foreign leaders while leading to cronyism and corruption at home. It is also painfully clear that we *aid* a number of countries that are not really our allies or friends. They have, in many cases, refused to cooperate and/or support us in simple matters and in international conflicts.

A 'zero-based' approach needs to be applied based on criteria that includes verifiable accounting of distributed aid and the reciprocal support of our international policies. Like the criteria applied to professional fund raisers here at home, let's make sure our 'aid' reaches the intended recipients. First let's look at 'humanitarian' aid and make sure substantially *all* of the aid reaches the victims. This means that we administer it – and not 'trust' anyone in a position to benefit personally. Second, 'economic' aid must contribute directly to promoting a free enterprise model – not any other theoretical economic system.

Let's also not assume that it is our responsibility or moral obligation to indefinitely bolster the economies of other countries. Even the exceptionalism[80] present in our society and country does not suggest that this makes sense.

---

[80] See **Exceptionalism**

# Genius

*"The essence of genius is to know what to overlook."*
*- William James*

*"Genius without education is like silver in the mine."*
*- Benjamin Franklin*

How is genius defined?

Is one's IQ number or Mensa qualification sufficient?

We've all known individuals that demonstrated profound understanding of difficult subjects but had difficulty with simple tasks. We've likewise known those with no formal education that were able to accomplish profound things. Is the dictionary definition as having '...exceptional intellectual or creative power or other natural ability..." sufficient?

The only reason for the inclusion of this subject in this book is the practical application of 'genius'. Can one see the Big Picture?[81] Does one solve problems or create them? Do they demonstrate common sense, leadership, and honesty?[82]

Before ascribing the qualities of 'genius' to anyone, make sure they possess more than academic credentials, positions of power, and/or impressive titles.

---

[81] See **Big Picture**
[82] See **Common Sense, Leadership, Honesty**

# Global Warming

*"Much of the debate over global warming is predicated on fear, rather than science."*
*-James Inhofe*

Some of the best examples of specious[83] statements and rhetorical speechmaking come from the advocates of Global Warming. Interestingly, most do not stand to gain financially from their evangelism, bringing into question why they enjoy inducing panic, scaring folks and stirring up ineffective crusades.

Using selective scientific facts, ignoring substantial evidence and totally dismissing common sense, these crusaders suggest that we can significantly impact our climate by changing light bulbs, buying carbon offsets, inflating tires, and purchasing hybrid cars. At best, these efforts stimulate new niche businesses – at worst, they lead consumers down totally ineffective paths of conservation.

The crusade worth participating in would be one of true conservation - reducing the waste of all of our resources. In reducing waste we save money personally and collectively, and preserve scarce resources usually without significant sacrifice of lifestyle. Whose budget couldn't use a reduction in electricity, gasoline, and heating expense?

---

[83] See **Specious**

# Goals

*"Define your goals in terms of the activities necessary to achieve them, and concentrate on those activities."*
*- Brian Tracy*

One characteristic of wildly successful individuals is the existence of personal goals. They may not always be obvious to others – and they may change frequently – but they exist. They may be modest or ambitious – they may be abstract or specific – but they exist!

Without goals, progress is not achieved and circumstances are not improved. Without goals, daily activities are determined by others, by surroundings, and by default activities. To achieve goals, change[84] is always required, and should be embraced!

*"Know what you want to do, hold the thought firmly, and do every day what should be done, and every sunset will see you that much nearer to your goal."*
*- Elbert Hubbard*

---

[84] See **Change**

# Grandiosity

*"...refers to an unrealistic sense of superiority - a sustained view of oneself as better than others..."*
*-Wikipedia*

As a first cousin of narcissism, grandiosity should be observed as a personality trait (or defect) present in many of the political and media arenas.

When so many of our information sources are rooted in grandiosity, it takes a real effort to sort out the rhetoric and self-serving statements delivered by politicians and media personalities.[85] Particularly frustrating is the logic (or lack of logic) and selective statistical reasoning[86] often put forth as factual.

Apply the smell test[87], and analyze for yourself the issues at hand.

---

[85] See **Demagogue, Specious Statements, Rhetoric**
[86] See **Comparative Rationalization**
[87] See **Smell Test**

# Green

*"The threat posed by humans to the natural environment is nothing compared to the threat to humans posed by global environmental policy."*

*- Fred Smith Jr.*

'Green' initiatives have been endlessly popularized as *good* just as automatically as profiling[88] has been made synonymous with *bad*. Let's discuss this a bit further.

Harming the environment in irreversible ways is definitely NOT green. However, short of creating a more elaborate definition, let's simplify the discussion by dividing 'green' into two categories.

The first is more properly labeled as *conservation*. We all embrace the concept that using non-renewable resources more rapidly than necessary is not a good idea. Conservation is using common sense to avoid waste.

Many proactive 'green' initiatives, however, fall into a category more appropriately labeled *'faux-green'*. These include hybrid cars and the conversion to non-incandescent light bulbs. The media and advertising-driven fervor that accompanies green campaigns often ignores the true costs of such efforts. Typically these green 'solutions' utilize less of one kind of 'fuel' – but may cost more in the long run, considering manufacturing, replacement cycles, (despite label promises) and require costly disposal procedures.

Exactly what have we saved? Clean electricity may be extremely inexpensive by comparison!

---

[88] See chapter on **Profiling**

# Gridlock

*"We have to stand up and claim our independence from the gridlock, from the partisanship, from the paralysis."*
*- Peter Hutchinson*

When grown men (and women) act like children, stamping their feet and gritting their teeth, and fail to see the 'big picture[89]', nothing is accomplished. When this group of adults is responsible for making decisions affecting millions of citizens, we've obviously chosen the wrong leaders!

We usually think of gridlock (as in traffic) as defined as by a large group of unmoving participants – where the cause and solution is unclear. In politics, the causes of and solutions to gridlock are not nearly so complex or ambiguous.

The causes usually originate with manifestations of power and control, augmented by stubbornness and a lack of compromise, culminating with a lack of common sense, responsibility, and creativity. (Note that I did not include a lack of common goals.)

The solution involves providing an incentive for achieving goals – just as in the free enterprise system! Pay for performance; bonuses for meeting goals; and terminations for failing or dishonesty. No business is constructed around employment guarantees for leaders, lifetime benefits or the absence of accountability requirements.

Isn't it time for our government to act like a responsible business – one that truly answers to its shareholders?

---

[89] See **Big Picture**

# Healthcare

The healthcare debate has multiple dimensions to challenge us.

1: Those who choose to be uninsured because of numerous 'safety nets' that will care for them. (entitlement mentality)

2: Those who believe they deserve the 'best' care money can buy but do nothing preventative or lifestyle-wise to help themselves. (cultural expectations)

3: Healthcare providers who play on cultural expectations but want 'no-risk' business models. (unrealistic)

4: A government that believes it can create 'universal' healthcare for everyone and run it better than the free enterprise system. (socialism)

5: A legal system that permits outrageous awards in cases of alleged malpractice. (corruption)

By no means will this chapter provide a comprehensive solution to the healthcare issues. No solution is suggested on these pages. However, a rational framework is proposed – with the expectation that an agreement on the goal will result in progress.

Culturally we have been raised to believe that healthcare (not just basic healthcare, but the ultimate in healthcare) is a right, a basic unalienable right, that all deserve. No 'class' limitations can be discussed because that would place more value on one person's life than another. No treatment limitations can be imposed because that would be to 'limit' the value of an individual human life. No limits on providers' fees or specific treatments can be discussed, because that removes the treatment decision-making from the medical professionals and places it in the hands of businessmen.

Creating a governmental agency to 'run' healthcare would guarantee additional expense, inefficiency, and corruption within the process. Regulating healthcare is, to a certain extent, responsible for today's situation. Additional regulation simply pushes us closer to a government-run system.

As unpopular as it will sound, several things must change. First, we will have to modify our personal expectations as to 'unlimited' healthcare treatment options. Second, we must all participate in reducing our healthcare risks – by employing preventative measures or forfeiting certain options. Third, medical providers, including hospitals, physicians and pharmaceutical companies will simply have to become more efficient, competitive, and depend less on subsidies and guarantees. Fourth, regulations restricting common sense business solutions between employers, insurance companies and healthcare providers must be removed. Fifth, individuals and families must participate in the risks and investment necessary to obtain health care. Where individual health savings accounts are implemented, and folks begin spending their own money instead of the money of others, more prudent decision-making takes place.

This all adds up to applying the law of supply and demand within the free enterprise system as the ultimate solution. With this goal in mind, the gradual removal of regulations and restrictions will allow a much better solution to evolve without governmental interference!

# Honesty

*"Whoever is careless with the truth in small matters cannot be trusted with important matters."*
*- Albert Einstein*

Where does one start when discussing honesty? Needless to say, hearing the truth is not always what we want to hear. Telling the truth is not always comfortable . . . and honesty doesn't always 'feel' like the best policy.

However, when the criteria for deciding whether telling the truth or lying is whether or not you get 'caught', our society has a dismal future ahead.

We can attack this issue on several levels . . . but the most egregious example is when elected leaders, trusted role models or employers are less than honest. It shakes our confidence at best, but tends to lower our standards and expectations at worst! As soon as we are found thinking or saying something like 'They all do it' - we are resigning our society to a moral abyss.

If you are satisfied that this is the best we can accomplish, stop reading. If you believe our society is capable of better, hold our leaders to a higher standard! Call them out when a promise made is not kept. With the currently available media and communications technology, no one can afford to fail in this area if citizens are vocal and tireless!

*"I have found that being honest is the best technique I can use. Right up front, tell people what you're trying to accomplish and what you're willing to sacrifice to accomplish it."*
*- Lee Iaccoca*

# Ideology

*"The uncontested absurdities of today are the accepted slogans of tomorrow. They come to be accepted by degrees, by dint of constant pressure on one side and constant retreat on the other - until one day when they are suddenly declared to be the country's official ideology."*
*- Ayn Rand*

By definition, ideology should be a '...set of ideas that make up one's goals, expectations and actions...'. Ideologies are all too often simply an assortment of abstract thoughts represented to be sacred guidelines for governing.

If today, we really believe that a given ideology should form the basis for economic or political policies, additional criteria must be met - i.e. ethics, efficiency, support from those governed, and reasonableness.

Before subscribing to a given ideology, the masses should be educated, experts should dissect it, individuals should debate it, and it should be *sold* [90] on its attributes over all alternatives. Ideology should be comprehensive in scope, embody common sense, and suggest concepts that are fair to and provide long-term benefits to all classes of society. Most importantly, no one should accept it simply because the media or elected leaders endorse it!

Do your own analysis! Apply your own values! Don't blindly accept the judgments of others!

*"Those looking for ideology in the White House should consider this: For the men who rule our world, rules are for other people."*
*- Naomi Klein*

---

[90] See **Salesmanship**

# Immigration & Borders

*"There is all the difference in the world between treating people equally and attempting to make them equal."*
- *F.A. Hayek*

It is irresponsible for the media and our elected leaders to talk at length about whether illegal immigrants should be granted amnesty, free health care, reduced college tuition and drivers licenses without discussing their 'illegal' status. This is a prime example of addressing symptoms – but not the problem!

The money and resources spent on these discussions and problems could have built a wall between the US and Mexico ten times over had our priorities been in the right place! For the most part, other countries respect our immigration laws and play by the rules – why is our policy not consistent? Sugar-coat the statistics any way you want to, our current toleration of illegal activities is *costing* this nation more than we can afford!

Building a wall - physical, electronic or otherwise, would significantly improve our federal, state and local budgetary problems, reduce crime and ultimately reduce the drug problems of our country. But . . . a fence isn't the only component. Start by enforcing existing laws. Second, punish employers who hire illegals. Award five years' probation and a hefty fine for a first offense. For the second offense, five years in prison; third offense, twenty years; fourth, throw away the key. Third, publicize the legal immigration process and precisely follow it. Problem solved!

With our resources, our ingenuity, and the right priorities, our borders could be secured within weeks!

# Innovation

*"Learning and innovation go hand in hand.*
*The arrogance of success is to think that what you did*
*yesterday will be sufficient for tomorrow."*
*- William Pollard*

Innovation is indisputably responsible for the incredible lifestyle we enjoy in this country. Without the innovation of creative minds and entrepreneurs – rewarded by the fruits of the free enterprise system – we would today resemble second and third world countries. If you enjoy the modern and efficient conveniences we enjoy, the technical sophistication of our transportation and communication devices, and so on, think about their origins!

The roots of innovation, creativity and learning almost certainly originate with our traditional family values and educational systems. These, plus the free enterprise system, are responsible for the incredible lifestyles available. Yet, various leaders and legislative efforts seem committed to degrading these traditions.

Anyone suggesting changes to these cultural resources should think twice. Bright, motivated, incentivized students are mandatory. Continued innovation is as essential going forward as it has been in the past. Any disincentives toward maintaining the traditional family structure or stifling the rewards for innovation, creativity or entrepreneurship would be very ill-advised.

Campaign for and support those leaders who espouse traditional values in domestic policy and reject the ideas that diminish the value of family, educational, and free enterprise initiatives. *NEVER* undervalue the importance of educating our youth. Celebrate those who are creative!

# Instant Gratification

*"Instant gratification is short-lived and full of regret."*
                                              *- Brenda Buster*

One of the results of our prosperity and successful societal development has been the expectations of many individuals that they should experience all of the 'creature-comforts' they observe others experiencing.[91] Teenagers observe the family lifestyle and expect that they should immediately be entitled to the same standard of living upon graduation from college. When the influence of television is added to the equation, the fantasies presented on-screen as 'reality' make it nearly impossible for young adults to balance 'efforts-required' with 'lifestyle-desired'.

The availability of easy tuition loans, the political bail-out mentality, the published job-placement salary statistics, and the constant bombardment of offers of 'delivery-now-pay-later' severely handicaps young adults.

Is it unreasonable to expect that we teach the concept of 'earned wealth'? Is it too late to introduce 'sweat-equity'?

---

[91] See **Entitlement**

# Intellectual Dishonesty

*"Intellectual dishonesty isn't a vice peculiar to any one group of people or another; it is a human problem.*
*But nowhere is it more salient than in the field of politics."*
-Jack Kerwick, Ph.D

The difference between intellectual dishonesty and intellectual incoherence is defined quite simply. Intellectual dishonesty is a strategy and tactic used when debating and/or discussing a controversial topic with others who disagree or are targets for persuasion. It is also the promotion of an idea known to be false.[92] Intellectual incoherence is the unfortunate circumstance where relatively bright people fall for and sincerely defend stupid ideas.

There is no better exhibition of intellectual dishonesty than in the debates of candidates for public office and the media interviews of the same candidates. The most common tactic among most candidates is to change the subject or refuse to answer the question. Close behind are the techniques of citing irrelevant issues, delivering negative innuendo, repeating baseless but popular slogans, repeating quotes out of context, denying truth based on 'technicalities', and comparative rationalization.[93] As inefficient moderators and interviewers are sucked into this routine, the debate often takes a totally unproductive direction.

While campaign managers and professional politicians would probably suggest this method to achieve a 'win', I would suggest constituents can slowly influence change by supporting those who deliver 'straight-talk' and honest dialogue!

---

[92] See **Specious Statements**
[93] See **Comparative Rationalization**

# Intellectual Incoherence

*"Few people are capable of expressing with equanimity opinions which differ from the prejudices of their social environment. Most people are even incapable of forming such opinions."*

*-- Albert Einstein*

The intellectual incoherence of our culture results from the inability or unwillingness of educated citizens to reason through everyday matters in order to see the obvious absurdity in the conclusions often drawn by others!

It is no surprise when uneducated folks fall for stupid ideas . . . but when our elite intellectuals do, it is a tragedy! The definition of 'incoherent' when coupled with the word 'intellectual' suggests that even bright people are often unable to create, express, and support coherent, organized, intelligent thoughts. It is obvious that possessing a high office, a high IQ or a PhD does not guarantee that one's intelligence will be utilized.

Since intellectuals are often taught to believe that they are superior, arrogance causes ideas to be defended when change is indicated. Another issue is hypocrisy – not wanting to practice or espouse what one knows because part of doing so would be unpleasant, unpopular or unprofitable. Often the issue is simply a belief system that results in denial.[94]

Recognize intellectual incoherence for what it is! A podium, a microphone, a news desk and/or a high office does not mean the words aren't fallacious![95]

---

[94] See **Change, Belief Systems** and **Denial**
[95] See **Specious Statements**

# Intelligence

*"What we think, or what we know, or what we believe is, in the end, of little consequence. The only consequence is what we do."*
                                                              *- John Ruskin*

A bit of history on the definition . . . the word 'intelligence' originally came from Latin - meant to 'discern'. Later philosophers preferred the word 'understand'. Even later, various researchers used 'good sense', 'problem-solving', and 'the ability to deal with cognitive complexity' to define intelligence.

Therefore, as a root concept of this book - we each need to use the above attributes to avoid being misled and unfairly influenced by those around us. We first need to apply the 'smell test' [96] to suggestions we hear - and then apply our own intelligence to analyzing the issue. Interestingly, the term 'Intellectually Incoherent' has been coined to describe those supporting unsustainable and irrational ideologies and exporting specious statements and speeches full of rhetorical language.

For far too long, popular and respected leaders have used rhetoric full of bad logic and lies to lead the masses. It is time to open our eyes and seek truth and reason. It is time to apply common sense to hypocrisy, perversion, deception, and lethal ideologies. It is simply NOT that complex to discern right from wrong, logic from faulty reasoning, and apply common sense! [97]

*"The test of a first-rate intelligence is the ability to hold two opposed ideas in the mind at the same time, and still retain the ability to function."*
                                                    *-- F. Scott Fitzgerald*

---

[96] See **Smell Test**
[97] See **Do Something Different**

# 'I Think'

Listen carefully to any news program, broadcast or cable, and count how many seconds go by before the on-air personality uses the words 'I think' . . . . or, better yet, count how many times the words 'I think' are repeated within any 30 minute segment! You will be astounded!

It is absolutely reprehensible how many 'newscasts' are, in fact, verbal editorial dissertations as opposed to news programs. The average viewer has no chance at all to distinguish between the 'reporting' of the news as opposed to the biased analysis of the events being revealed! Responsible reporting (or a program labeled as 'news') would never use the 'I think' phrase.

Along with 'I Think' are similar specious phrases – 'You Know' & 'They Say'. 'You Know' implies that you should already believe what follows – and without defining who 'They' are, whatever 'They' said is meaningless.

It's no wonder the general public has difficulty forming beliefs based on facts. Even the largest 'news' organizations deliver more airtime 'editorializing' than reporting! This practice alone, combined with selective reporting and repetitiveness, has absolutely positioned the media[98] to form beliefs[99] and opinions in the minds of the masses!

*"What you hear repeatedly you will eventually believe."*

*- Michael Korda*

---

[98] See **Media**
[99] See **Belief Systems**

# Jobs vs. Careers

*"The biggest mistake that you can make is to believe that you are working for someone else. Job security is gone, the driving force of a career must come from the individual, remember: jobs are owned by the company, you own your career."*
*- Earl Nightingale*

It is difficult to say it any better. Today's employer-employee relationship is different than it was a generation ago. The old paternalistic culture has given way to a self-directed one. As in most of life's endeavors, depending on someone else to 'take care of you' is not a productive strategy.

Setting individual goals[100], acting on those goals, and becoming your own best salesman[101] will result in the career you enjoy.

Being able to do what you most enjoy and be rewarded monetarily for doing it is the definition of a great career!

*"You've achieved success in your field when you don't know whether what you're doing is work or play."*
*- Warren Beatty*

---

[100] See **Goals**
[101] See **Salesmanship**

# Justice System

*"Law is not justice and a trial is not a scientific inquiry into truth.
A trial is the resolution of a dispute."*

*- Edison Haines*

We should probably rename this chapter the 'Legal System' because justice is not really the dominant concept being pursued. While we collectively would like to believe that this institution, with all of its sacred halls and robes, is highly principled, fair and beyond reproach, it would be naive to do so.

Money, expediency, and compromise are the most significant components of this system and don't let anyone persuade you otherwise. Perhaps it would be better described as the 'attorneys-full-employment-system'. Why do we allow frivolous lawsuits without any merit whatsoever to bleed dollars from innocent defendants? Why do insurance companies settle when there is clearly no liability? Without money the system is not accessible, excessive money often allows justice to be bypassed, and money is all too often substituted for justice! The real scandal is that the system allows individuals to impose heavy expenses on others with no investment of their own. This leads to significant legalized extortion!

Instituting a loser-pays[102] system with some reasonable tort reform solves most of the issues immediately and automatically – and keeps it simple. Insist on it with your candidates!

---

[102] See **Loser Pays**

# Kool-Aid (Drinking the...)

> *" 'Drinking the Kool-Aid' means becoming a firm believer in something: accepting an argument, philosophy or social norm wholeheartedly or blindly without critical examination."*
> *- Wikipedia*

As unfortunate as it is that this phrase had such a tragic origin, the example, nevertheless, is graphic and clear. Those who accept and believe without applying their intelligence and judgment are naïve and destined for disappointment if not outright failure.

The premise of this book is partially summed up in this concept – if you accept the attitudes and perspectives of the media, your union or your friends, without critically examining its validity and compatibility with your value system, you are guilty of 'Drinking the Kool-Aid'. This means that you are resigning yourself to the values and belief systems of others, whether smart or shallow. Worse than that, you are submitting to their manipulation and supporting ***their*** cause!

Listening to the advice and promises of our candidates and leaders, following without questioning, and accepting whatever is delivered, means you are not using your innate intelligence! The need for independent thinking and preemptive actions has never been greater.

Maintaining a passive stance on issues that will affect your future is resigning yourself to less-than-optimum conditions. Assuming that others will look out for your interests is naïve. Remember, you can either be part of the solution or remain part of the problem!

# Leadership

*"Leadership is action, not position."*
*- Donald H. McGannon*

Leadership is not about making speeches or being liked . . . it is about achieving results through others. It is about having people becoming more confident by watching your decision-making. It is about earning respect without asking for or demanding it. It is about results, not promises.

Volumes have been written about leadership techniques, leadership attributes and leadership methods[103] . . . but the short version is that true leadership qualities are usually not 'learned'. They are an inherent part of personality, a combination of learned and observed behaviors, and result from upbringing, role models and education.

- Honest leaders make good policies in the open, never in closed sessions.

- True leaders must be willing to do unpopular things when necessary for the common good.

- Strong leaders must have strength and conviction . . and they will not be forgiven for NOT deciding.

- Effective leaders create a sense of urgency for change through communication and persuasion.

- Sincere leaders evoke a common commitment to shared values.

- Efficient leaders accomplish significant results by enlisting others to work toward a common goal

---

[103] See **Simplification**

# Listening

*"The biggest communication problem is that
we do not listen to understand.
We listen to reply."*
*- unknown*

There is little that can be said to elaborate on this concept. Successful people are skillful in listening – and responding in a manner that achieves objectives. Without first listening, inadequate responses are given, extending the time required to accomplish the results desired!

Politicians are notorious for providing non-responsive answers to questions – choosing instead to deliver predetermined statements on predetermined subjects – purely to achieve *their* goals, not the goals of the interviewer or their constituency.

Beware of non-listeners – they are not considering what you are saying!

*"There are people who, instead of listening to what is being said
to them, are already listening to what they are going
to say themselves."*
*-- Albert Guinon*

# Literacy

*"The illiterate of the 21st century will not be those who cannot read and write, but those who cannot learn, unlearn, and relearn."*
*-- Alvin Toffler*

A civilized society expecting to prosper must rely on the good judgement and actions of its citizens. The components of good judgement involve values, education, experience and intelligence. The components of good actions include good judgement, motivation and opportunity.

The environment(s) in which we are raised and live are largely responsible for how literate we become. Fortunate are those who come from homes where well-rounded and balanced daily practices result in literate young adults. Judging from typical man-on-the-street interviews, many voting, procreating adults today are sorely lacking in practical literacy. We see disappointing voids in their knowledge of current events, technology, basic economic principles and even many factors directly influencing their daily lives.

By the time most reach adulthood, attitudes toward learning and re-learning are often fixed – and do not progress. Assisting those around us to adapt, welcome change, and continuously learn new things would benefit everyone!

# Logic

*"An opinion should be the result of thought, not a substitute for it."*

*- Jef Mallett*

Technically, logic is the method by which we form opinions based on facts. However, choosing which facts to consider or discard in reaching an opinion often leads to flawed conclusions. Logically reasoned statements are normally 'true' assuming that the underlying facts and assumptions are complete and correct.

Confused enough?

Regardless of the relationship you may assign between the words 'Opinion', 'Facts', 'Truth', and 'Logic', the point to be made is that while everyone has a 'right' to their 'opinion', not all opinions are equally valid. Many opinions are developed completely based on very passive listening to someone else expressing an opinion. One's personal resistance to change[104] is a very critical component in accepting or rejecting the opinions of others. One's belief system[105] strongly influences what one *wants* to believe. The passionate delivery of political dialogue[106] is a powerful factor in forming opinions among the masses. Mass media bias influences are indisputable.

The point is that, without personal research and analysis by an intelligent mind, (independent rationality) one succumbs to the conclusions of others – who may have very different beliefs and motivations. Make sure you are thinking for yourself!

---

[104] See **Change**
[105] See **Belief Systems**
[106] See **Specious Statements, Rhetoric**

# Loser Pays

*"According to the law of nature it is only fair that no one should become richer through damages and injuries suffered by another."*
*- Marcus Tullius Cicero*

Our legal system could be improved very quickly if the 'loser pays' concept were applied. Today's system allows virtually anyone to file a lawsuit for almost any reason - with or without ANY evidence of wrongdoing or neglectful behavior - forcing those sued to spend considerable money to defend themselves. Far too many suits are frivolous - meaning that there is no evidence of wrongdoing or liability. Sadly, plaintiffs often obtain legal help on a contingency basis (meaning they have no investment in the process) and the attorneys involved know that certain tactics will elicit a 'payout' even when no legitimate fault is found - because the 'system' causes innocent defendants (or their insurance companies) to pay - just to terminate (settle) the action.

This practice consumes enormous amounts of money on both sides - but would be all but eliminated if the plaintiff and/or their attorneys had to pay the expenses of the innocent party sued if no fault was found. The United States is virtually the only civilized country NOT to have adopted this system!

If 'loser-pays' was implemented, both parties would work much harder to achieve win-win solutions and only a small fraction of the lawsuits filed today would happen. The only potential losers would be those attorneys who milk the system, exploiting system deficiencies to line their pockets. Persuade your state and federal legislators to make 'loser-pays' law of the land!

# Mistakes

*"No one who cannot rejoice in the discovery of
his own mistakes deserves to be called a scholar."*
*-- Donald Foster*

Learning from mistakes is undeniably a powerful tool in maturing and becoming more productive. We've all grown up reciting tired expressions about 'falling and getting up' that support this learning technique.

How we respond to our mistakes and to the mistakes of others is both a measure of maturity and honesty. It is difficult to respect leaders who find it impossible to admit mistakes and insist on rationalizing bad decisions.[107]

Not only should we demonstrate our willingness to admit mistakes, but we should celebrate those who are able to publicly and vocally demonstrate that they are continuing to learn from theirs!

---

[107] See **Comparative Rationalization**

# Media

*"When the only values in communication are market share, ratings, and profit, all communication becomes pornography; not necessarily sexual in nature but appealing to our baser instincts and prurient interests. From the actual sex in movies, music and ads, to gratuitous violence, to the fake news that panders to ideological outrage on all sides, all we do now is titillate and excite rather than educate and inform.*
*It simply makes us angrier and less knowledgeable."*
*- Stephen Smith*

The pure, raw, undisputed power of the media is downright scary. The minds of virtually everyone – including our legislators – are influenced more by the printed and broadcast media than anything else. What is printed and/or spoken, whether verified or not, is routinely consumed as factual. All too often, the pressures of deadlines, the pursuit of market share, 'exclusivity' claims and so forth shortcut the validation process. Add bias to this and what we have is the most powerful attitude-forming machine on earth!

The role of a reporter or journalist should be to '… collect, verify, and report information . . .' We should insist that there be a clear line between reporting and 'editorializing', where opinions are expressed and bias injected. Today, this 'clear line' has all but disappeared. Either through inertia or directive, virtually all reporting is delivered in a clearly biased style.

In covering the election season, the press over-analyzes every spoken hiccup and minuscule statistical change in questionable polls, leading to additional biased reporting. With the persuasive power of electronic delivery of photos, graphics, and live video, the average viewer is hard pressed to doubt the concepts presented.

The effect of all this is to make it seem as if something monumental is happening even when it isn't[108] – and vice versa – effectively 'telling' the masses what they should be concerned about and what they should ignore.

This is the opposite of what the media should be doing and the trend is getting worse with each passing year. During the election season, for example, pundits and analysts are inserted into newscasts with regularity, totally obscuring the factual portions of the stories. Current events are reported differently depending on the competing stories of the day. Advice is given by non-authorities but accepted by the non-thinking emotional masses due to the 'bully-pulpit' status of the press.

I see no cure unless citizens refuse to subscribe. Demanding unbiased coverage is very unlikely to significantly impact policies due to the traditions and momentum of established outlets. Supporting startup entities is difficult since advertisers buy based on market share and sheer numbers of readers/listeners.

A very basic change in the responses of intelligent citizenry is essential when polled, when engaged in social conversations, and in communication with leaders, both public and private. The expression of and insistence on common sense needs to pervade all serious conversation about our governance and society.

*"The news is not about news anymore. It's about protecting some people, destroying others and shoving a socialist agenda down the collective throats of America."*
*-Charlie Daniels*

*"Whoever controls the media, controls the mind."*
*- Jim Morrison*

---

[108] See **Drama Queens**

# Natural Laws

*'A law or body of laws that derives from nature and is believed to be binding upon human actions apart from or in conjunction with laws established by human authority.'*

To succeed in life or in business there are some natural laws that apply. Taking issue with these 'natural' laws is a form of denial and very counterproductive! The next time you are tempted to pursue a 'too-good-to-be-true' offer, think again. The world has more than enough folks that are waiting for their fortune to be realized by some big 'deal' that will come along. When your boss or your elected representative doesn't subscribe to these natural principles, look for another!

- **Profit is good**
  whether in government, business or your home budget

- **You get what you pay for**
  bargains are temporary

- **There is no free lunch**
  nothing is free, and we'd all be wise to believe this

- **A satisfied customer is your most valuable asset**
  whether in business or the public sector

- **Under-promise and over-deliver**
  a principle that everyone would be wise to follow!

- **Supply and demand**
  self-regulating, maximizes efficiency, delivers best value

# Noise

*Sound . . . of a loud, harsh, or confused kind:*
*deafening noise . . . a random and persistent disturbance, that*
*obscures or reduces the clarity of a signal . . . Extraneous,*
*irrelevant, or meaningless facts, information, statistics, etc.*

The 'over-reporting' of certain news stories is the equivalent of 'noise' – by the definition above. When the majority of media time and newsprint is consumed with emotional tripe and void of intelligent discussion about the most important issues of the day, our citizenry is unfairly guided toward the avoidance of critical topics. It is virtually impossible to focus on long term issues when such emotional energy is consumed on items such as a celebrity affair, a sports figure's salary, the trial of a drama queen, a candidate's quote out of context, or bedbugs.

Noise is distracting, diverting and a waste of energy and talent. Let's begin by suggesting to the press, our professors, ministers and entertainers that some sort of re-prioritization needs to take place.

# OCD (Obsessive Compulsive Disorder)

*"Politics is perhaps the only profession for which
no preparation is thought necessary."*
            *-- Robert Louis Stevenson*

It seems that our national leadership is exhibiting the classic signs of Obsessive Compulsive Disorder.

1. Performing repetitive behaviors that don't make sense.

2. Becoming upset when interrupted in an activity

3. Preoccupation with a useless, time consuming activity

4. Constantly asking for reassurance

5. Claiming to be unable to do things previously accomplished

How is it possible that we have elected so many leaders that collectively exhibit this kind of behavior - doing ineffective things over and over . . . becoming upset when a suggestion is made that we should 'do something different' [109] . . . and defending gridlocked[110] practices?

The only result possible from this condition is the continued decay of our economic system and our enviable quality of life. Common sense dictates that we elect some plain-speaking, capable, common-sense-driven leaders who are not afraid to implement real changes rather than debate the symptoms of our problems.

The beginning of reform in our government must start at a grassroots level – with dissatisfied, proactive citizens!

---

[109] See **Do Something Different**
[110] See **Gridlock**

# Overrated

### Global Warming

Regardless of the causes or the perceived severity of the problem, one thing is clear:   none of the currently popular 'solutions' have any chance of effecting any significant change.

### Green

The vast majority of 'green' initiatives presented to consumers are marketing hype without substantive conservation or economic benefits.

### Hybrid cars

Really?  Look at the overall costs and fuel consumption statistics compared to conventional economy vehicles.  Again, it is marketing hype to suck in consumers who don't think for themselves!  (Do you really believe that a chrome 'hybrid' label on your SUV's tailgate will save the world - or impress your intelligent neighbors?)

### New Technology Light Bulbs

Another example of congress listening to incoherent lobbyists who suggest that consuming a few less watts solves all of the energy problems of the country. Look at the overall costs, the disposal issues, the low performance and unrealistic longevity claims!

### Airport Security

Like locks on doors, such measures keep the honest people honest and barely annoy the criminals.

# Perseverance

*"Perseverance is the hard work you do after you get tired
of doing the hard work you already did."*
*- Newt Gingrich*

It is difficult to deliver a persuasive argument that convinces today's workforce that strenuous efforts are necessary to achieve above-average results. There are too many examples where it appears (accurately or inaccurately) that fortunes were made with no visible 'strenuous' effort. Admittedly, some entrepreneurs were 'at the right place at the right time' and it was easier than usual – but most expended considerable perseverance and effort in achieving exceptional results.

Many graduates mail resumes and then sit back and wait . . . . believing they've done their part and expecting job offers to 'arrive'. This author suggests that 'good things may come to those who wait – but only those things left behind by those who hustle!'

*"Opportunity is missed by most people because it is dressed in
overalls and looks like work."*
*- Thomas A. Edison*

# Philosophy

*"There's a difference between a philosophy and a bumper sticker."*
*-- Charles M. Schulz*

As we drive, we observe folks who are compelled to place bumper stickers on their cars to advertise a current position, attitude or other priority they hold. Some are serious, some amusing, while others suggest reasonably profound philosophical beliefs and attitudes.

It's unfortunate that all can't result in conversation that could lead to intelligent change. Just imagine what could result from a productive debate on some of the subjects!

Could our literacy level be raised?[111]

Could minds be changed?[112]

Could politics be seriously discussed and candidates qualified?[113]

*"There is nobody so irritating as somebody with less intelligence and more sense than we have."*
*-- Don Herold*

---

[111] See **Literacy**
[112] See **Change**
[113] See **Representative Government**

# Political Correctness

*"Just because you're offended doesn't mean you're in the right."*
*-Ricky Gervais*

The concept that language, ideas, policies, and behavior should minimize social and institutional offense in occupational, gender, racial, cultural, sexual orientation, disability, and age-related contexts is flawed. If all views and attitudes should be considered as equally valid, why do those who embrace this point of view feel the need to push their agenda as the "correct" one while at the same time demonizing other views as "incorrect"?

Do we really believe that everyone is better served if no one is ever offended? Do we have the 'right'[114] to never be slighted or hurt? What constitutes offensiveness? One individual complaining? The sensitivities of some individuals would prevent any holiday decorations, any single-language signage, and any heterosexual displays of affection! Differences are to be recognized and respected – but this does not mean undiscussed or unlabeled.

To render art, commerce and religious displays to be totally non-offensive would mean their elimination. To eliminate all potentially offensive words renders our communication ineffective.

We all have eyes that we can close, televisions we can turn off and ears that be tuned out. We can all walk away.

*"He who dares not offend cannot be honest"*
*-Thomas Paine*

---

[114] See **Rights vs. Responsibilities**

# Politics

*"Politics is the conspiracy of the unproductive but organized against the productive but unorganized."*
*- Joseph Sobran*

It is difficult to more accurately characterize the political system in our country than the quotes on this page do. Without intending to be cynical or sarcastic, read each of these and attempt to make an argument against them!

*"Politics, n. Strife of interests masquerading as a contest of principles."*
*-- Ambrose Bierce*

Arguably, our system has resulted in a more prosperous and viable environment than any other – but it may be time to seriously question its sustainability. There are many indications that we may not be able continue the prosperous trends we enjoy today. Are our leaders [115] intelligently planning for the future or are they dealing only with the challenges of today? Do they have true accountability?[116] Do they even exhibit common sense?[117]

*"It is hard to imagine a more stupid or more dangerous way of making decisions than by putting those decisions in the hands of people who pay no price for being wrong."*
*-Thomas Sowell*

*"Bureaucracy is a sickening beast for people with innate common sense"*
*- Stan Otts*

---

[115] See **Bureaucrats**
[116] See **Accountability**
[117] See **Common Sense**

# Populism

*"The struggle between ordinary people
and a self-serving undemocratic elite."*
                                    *- Steve Stark*

One definition of populism is the ongoing war of ideology between the masses and the elite – with the assumption that there are no common objectives or reasons to co-exist. Many factors enter into this argument – including one's belief system, the current status of society's entitlement programs, the number of unemployed, and general economic conditions.

The factual arguments are constantly mixed with the emotional arguments and everyday dishonest rhetoric totally clouds the issue. The words 'class warfare' used by the media – and adopted by politicians – further incites irrational behavior. The entitlement-seeking class is led to believe that their 'rights' are threatened and that the 'rights' of the elite should be modified.

The fact is that our country does not impose *any* restrictions on 'class' mobility. Everyone has the opportunity to elevate themselves. Income groups or 'classes' are not fixed. Individual initiatives are required – and there is no substitute for hard work and an intelligent strategy. The premise that 'the rich live off the poor' and that the poor are 'stuck' in their circumstance is simply not true.

# Posturing

*"There are people who think that everything one does
with a serious face is sensible."*
*-- Georg Christoph Lichtenberg*

Posturing[118] is defined as behaving in a way intended to impress or mislead others. I might add the word 'persuade' - which can be either bad or good, depending on the motives of the presenter.

Listening to a typical politician is 90% posturing and 10% information. A similar ratio exists with the national media.

What is wrong with this picture? As described in the introduction to this book, it has become increasingly important that each of us use our intelligence to dissect, analyze, and draw our own conclusions. Unfortunately, the majority of politicians spend far too much of their time shamelessly promoting personal agendas - not representing their constituents. The media is pursuing market share, often by stressing the sensational and promoting politicians who will enhance their business models.

Accepting at face value the words of a newscaster or politician is to buy what they are selling without question! Challenging their positions with your own intelligent analysis is both responsible and positive!

*"When you want to help people, you tell them the truth. When you
want to help yourself, you tell them what they want to hear."*
*-Thomas Sowell*

---

[118] Se chapters on **Specious Statements, Kool-Aid, Salesmanship**

# Principles

*"When one bases his life on principle,*
*99 percent of his decisions are already made."*
*- Author Unknown*

According to Wikipedia, principles are '. . . a set of values that orientate and rule the conduct of a concrete society. . .'

True leaders are guided by principles – a combination of personal, moral, and ethical values that form the basis of good decision-making that subsequently benefits the total of society.

The question that remains is why we use a political process that is seemingly void of the influence of principles to choose our leaders. Once in office, expediency, cronyism, deal-making, and manipulation govern virtually all voting and policy making. The lack of ethical principles leads to the lack of transparency[119] and the lack of business principles[120] leads to fiscal irresponsibility.

When the primary motivator for principled behavior is the fear of getting caught,[121] we will have fully committed to the moral decay of our culture!

Remind yourself and your elected leaders that there are always choices to make – between doing the right thing and doing the most expeditious. Principles should make that choice very easy.

*"There are three constants in life... change, choice and principles."*
*- Stephen R. Covey*

---

[119] See **Transparency**
[120] See **Budgets**
[121] See **Character**

# Priorities

*"Action expresses priorities."*
*- Mohandas Gandhi*

Few of us are able to accomplish everything we'd like to accomplish. Even the most organized leaders with efficient, organized staffs must choose which objectives to pursue and which to delay. It's a matter of setting priorities!

We become dysfunctional when priorities are set without regard for importance, we procrastinate, or we announce what is important but indicate otherwise by our actions.[122] In personal decisions, the consequences may not impact others – but in one's professional life or in public leadership positions, the consequences impact many others.

There are issues that are important but not urgent, issues that are urgent but not important, issues that are important AND urgent - and of course, issues that are not important or urgent. Knowing how to assign the correct label and prioritize is the mark of truly effective leaders. The same applies to individuals in accomplishing everyday tasks!

True leaders demonstrate proficiency in setting priorities. Get rid of those who do only what is easiest, most politically expedient, or whatever the media labels as urgent.

It's time we prioritize our interaction with our public leaders – they've gone far too long in pursuit of their own agendas.

---

[122] See **Actions Speak Louder than Words**

# Private Enterprise

*"Some see private enterprise as a predatory target to be shot, others as a cow to be milked, but few are those who see it as a sturdy horse pulling the wagon."*

*- Winston Churchill*

Any honest historian analyzing the prosperity and growth of our society cannot deny the absolute and primary role private enterprise has played.

Likewise, any honest politician who suggests that more government oversight will improve on the natural laws [123] governing private enterprise and the free enterprise system is not in touch with reality.

The free enterprise system, and its backbone of private enterprise, holds the greatest potential for solving social and economic challenges of almost all types. It is self-regulating, internally motivated, and governed by natural laws that assure responsiveness, quality, competition and creativity.

---

[123] See **Natural Laws**

# Privatization

*"The private sector is motivated by profit and efficiency and the US government often is not."*

*- Eric Anderson*

Privatization is the process of transferring the ownership and/or operation of a program or activity from the public sector to the private sector. The fact that this process has a formal 'label', is widely discussed, and frequently implemented gives credence to the fact that private enterprise is often more efficient and productive than public administration.

The reason is simple – motivation. Public officials, whether elected or appointed are rarely entrepreneurial in their leadership characteristics. By observation, public servants are not usually risk-takers or highly competitive. In most cases, they would be unable to explain and defend the necessity of profit in their budgeting process. Of course there are rare exceptions.

The natural laws that govern the free enterprise system are wonderfully self-regulating and, without intervention, provide efficiency and productivity to worthy enterprises. Obviously inefficient governmental programs are prime candidates for privatization. Other than reducing the size of our bloated bureaucracy, there is no downside!

# Productivity

*"Productivity and the growth of productivity must be the first economic consideration at all times, not the last. That is the source of technological innovation, jobs, and wealth."*
*- William E. Simon*

The definition is simple – the ratio of input compared to output! In business – particularly in manufacturing - productivity is what defines relative success. Firms with the lowest labor and material costs vs. sales are the most successful. Personally, productivity is a comparison of effort vs. results.

Why is productivity a worthy chapter in this book? Like it or not, we are all participants in one or more production undertaking. Whether it is building something in a factory or cooking the daily family meals at home, we should all be conscious of how to accomplish *more* with *less*! Improving our personal and/or business productivity contributes significantly to happiness, satisfaction, and wealth.

In government, the same rules apply. Regulations that inhibit productivity should be abolished. Unions that preach work slow-downs should be criminally prosecuted.

It's been said that *'wealth'* is when small efforts produce large results . . . and that *'poverty'* is when large efforts produce small results.

What more needs to be said?

# Profiling

*. . . the inclusion of all observed characteristics in determining whether a person is considered likely to commit a particular type of crime or an illegal act or to behave in a "predictable" manner. . .*

Who decided that 'profiling' was a bad thing?

By definition, profiling is the practice of collecting data that predicts a behavior. We do it with weather forecasting, psychology, criminal forensics, and child rearing. Why is it, all of a sudden, wrong when it comes to preventing hijacking or terrorism when the consequences are much more severe? This is carrying political correctness,[124] a seriously questionable practice, to the point of absurdity.

Continuing to classify this as a 'bad' concept will render law enforcement ineffective, education incomplete and international negotiations unproductive. It will also destroy all semblance of safety within our society. The only segments of society potentially 'injured' by profiling are the segments that have been historically responsible for a disproportionate share of the crimes we are trying to prevent.

If 'profiling' effectively prevents these crimes, are we not logically and efficiently achieving our objective while 'inconveniencing' the minimum number of our citizens?

Think and decide for yourself . . . instead of automatically believing everything you've heard!

---

[124] See chapter on 'Political Correctness'

# Profit

*"The worst crime against working people is a company
which fails to operate at a profit."*
**-Samuel Gompers**

Like some of the 'natural laws' discussed earlier, profitability is a good thing. It is one of the 'natural laws'.[125] Profit, quite simply, is generating more income than expense, which means having a positive balance at the bottom of one's checkbook, - not spending more than you take in - as an individual, a corporation or a governmental agency.

Although it may seem like beating a dead horse, the result of NOT being profitable is failure; it means going out of business - it means unsustainability.

Why then do political leaders pretend that they have a secret that supersedes this natural law? It has never worked - and never will!

If your favorite candidate cannot explain why profitability is absolutely mandatory, find another. If your elected official doesn't insist on a balanced budget in every agency he or she governs, ask them why!

---

[125] See **Natural Laws**

# Promises

*"You know, to address crowds and make promises does not require very much brains."*

*- Eduard Shevardnadze*

A leader deserving of respect understands what a promise is - and doesn't make commitments that he can't keep. In politics, unfortunately, being truthful is not a real priority and, as a result, promises flow freely and promises are rarely 'kept'. Admittedly, the pressure of 'doing what it takes to win'[126] convinces most political strategists that rhetoric and specious statements are appropriate.

To ask why this condition exists is rather basic. It exists because we, as constituents, tolerate this behavior. It exists because our values have eroded to the point that we don't see such behavior as unacceptable. The famous shrugging-of-shoulders gesture indicating that we feel powerless to do anything about it or, worse yet, that we find empty promises acceptable suggests that we don't expect change.

To continue down this path is to commit to decaying societal values. Eventually it will reduce our great society to that of a third world entity. Only with renewed active citizenship will it change!

---

[126] See **Actions Speak Louder than Words**

# Reputation

*"You can't build a reputation on what you are going to do. "*

*-- Henry Ford*

Similar to natural laws [127] and the free enterprise system [128], reputations are created as a *result* of good decisions and actions, not artificial or contrived activities. Attempts to inflate or change reputations are short-lived at best.

Leaders who don't 'practice what they preach' and believe that the rules are different for those that 'make the rules' than for everyone else are doomed to create poor reputations among astute observers.

Everyone should be challenged to form assessments of leaders independent of polls, media surveys, and popular opinion. Observe actions – compare to promises and words – and define one's reputation based on your observation and fact-finding, not the opinions of others.

---

[127] See **Natural Laws**
[128] See **Free Enterprise System**

# Regulation

*"It's so much easier to suggest solutions*
*when you don't know too much about the problem."*
*-Malcolm Forbes*

America is drowning in red tape, which is choking the entrepreneurial spirit of small businesses and hampering job creation. The best way to get the economy moving again is to reduce the regulatory burden imposed on private enterprise by misguided and overbearing federal bureaucrats.

The idea that the federal government and state governments can more efficiently operate *anything* has long been proven to be fantasy.[129] Likewise, attempts to regulate details that are better 'regulated' by natural laws[130] have also proven to fail in the long term.

Businessmen know more about building profitable businesses long-term than politicians; Teachers know more about education than bureaucrats; and Consumers can drive product safety, pricing, distribution and labeling as well as public servants.

---

[129] See **Privatization**
[130] See **Natural Laws**

# Respect

Respect variously describes a level of esteem, a mode of treatment, and/or a level of toleration of others. Demonstrating proper respect is a skill, an art, and an indication of maturity. There are several types of 'respect'.

Respect is first observed where there is an age difference (children toward adults, adults toward the elderly etc.)

The second type of respect is created by one's position (as supervisors, law enforcement personnel, elected officials etc.).

Third, there is 'earned' respect. The 'earned' level of respect is afforded to someone because of the way they conduct themselves, the knowledge they have, or their achievements and accomplishments.

Individuals who 'demand' respect without 'earning' it are delusional. They may command a loyalty or following - but without earning it, such a following will be temporary. If readers follow the suggestions in this book, leaders who demand respect without earning it will receive their just reward eventually!

# Rhetoric

*"Rhetoric is the art of ruling the minds of men."*
*- Plato*

As compared with specious statements, rhetoric shares the persuasive and impression-making characteristics but is simply lacking in meaningful content. Because rhetoric rarely identifies sincere objectives, its differences from specious statements are marginal.

Most often heard from those 'selling' something but lacking in substance, rhetorical language sounds good, presents seemingly plausible ideas and gets your head to start nodding 'yes' - but totally fails in accomplishing anything! You can quickly identify those who fit this definition.

A response of 'BS' is totally accurate - even if inappropriate!

We are presented with idiotic theories, beliefs, and opinions on a daily basis. Some have achieved credibility[131] without having any critical thinking or sufficient rational analysis applied.

Enter common sense. Use your intelligence to 'see through' the rhetoric. Use your reasoning ability to identify those with ulterior motives. Question the appearance of sincerity when the actions and follow-through are missing. Independently pursue a rational analysis. Be vocal with your 'BS' responses!

---

[131] See **Global Warming**

# Right Thing (doing the)

*"What we think, or what we know, or what we believe is, in the end, of little consequence. The only consequence is what we do."*

*- John Ruskin*

This book is, among other things, a prescription for improving our society and culture. Following some or all of the suggestions made here WILL improve relationships, reduce waste, increase productivity and result in more rational relationships.

Having said that, it is often as simple as '...doing the right thing...'. Plus, doing the right thing is often the easiest to determine and implement!

Historically, *virtually all* of the philosophers, religious leaders, teachers, writers, and wise thinkers embody the 'Golden Rule' in their advice in one form or another . . . and I defy anyone to provide an improved version!

Rotary International, the well-respected service organization with service clubs around the world, has a well-known and long respected 4-way test that makes it simple:

**1. Is it the TRUTH?**

**2. Is it FAIR to all concerned?**

**3. Will it build GOODWILL and BETTER FRIENDSHIPS?**

**4. Will it be BENEFICIAL to all concerned?**

Do to others what you would want them to do to you! No if's, and's or but's. It's a prescription you may laugh at - but I challenge you to come up with a better solution!

# Rights vs. Responsibilities

*"Liberty and responsibility are inseparable. A free society will not function or maintain itself unless its members regard it as right that each individual occupy the position that results from his action and accept it as due to his own action."*

*- F.A. Hayek*

You've all met them – individuals who scream loudly that they have the 'right' to do something they haven't done on their own, or be given something they can't obtain on their own. 99% percent of the time, they are screaming about their 'rights' because they have failed to reach their desired social status or lifestyle through their own actions – and expect someone else to provide for them.

When someone screams about rights, you can bet they are expecting something for nothing or evading their common sense role in solving the problem. Rights are often confused with entitlements[132] which, unfortunately, have become pervasive.

Rights are not a substitute for hard work, poor decision-making or misfortune. 'Rights' should never enable one to penalize others. When one says, 'I'm going to call my lawyer' or 'I'm going to sue you,[133] walk away. There is no point in encouraging this behavior!

*"We must reject the idea that every time a law's broken, society is guilty rather than the lawbreaker. It is time to restore the American precept that each individual is accountable for his actions."*

*-Ronald Regan*

---

[132] See **Entitlements**
[133] See **Judicial System**

# Representative Government

*"We'd all like to vote for the best man, but he's never a candidate."*
*- Frank McKinney "Kin" Hubbard*

Despite the cynicism of the quote above, the unfortunate truth is that our current governmental environment discourages many qualified individuals from seeking public office. Note that I said the current 'environment', not the governmental 'structure'. We have an excellent framework for responsible governance provided the officeholders are principled, ethical and hard-working.

The beginning of the problem is the tolerance by the citizenry of the dishonest manipulation of the system by those elected. Earmarks, [134] cronyism, [135] and the pursuit of personal agendas totally overshadow the 'real' responsibility of our elected representatives, *representing their constituents!*

There should be no tolerance of closed-door meetings; no piggybacking of unrelated legislation; and no restrictions on CSPAN-style broadcasting of all sessions and meetings. If your representative promised transparency as a candidate and doesn't insist on this – recall him immediately!

*"It is inaccurate to say that I hate everything. I am strongly in favor of common sense, common honesty, and common decency. This makes me forever ineligible for public office."*
*- H. L. Mencken*

---

[134] See **Earmarks**
[135] See **Cronyism**

# Rudeness

*"Rudeness is the weak man's imitation of strength."*
*-- Eric Hoffer*

Along with the old adage – that you catch more flies with honey than with vinegar – it stands to reason that one gains more cooperation with politeness than with rudeness. However contrary to emotional leanings, to be respected and valued as opposed to being feared, is a sign of maturity and strength.

True leaders [136] accomplish real goals through persuasion, not through intimidation. Respect [137] is earned, not demanded. Well-mannered folks will always win long-term when compared with rude folks.

---

[136] See **Leadership**
[137] See **Respect**

# Salesmanship

One of the greatest injustices of our educational system is the absence of coursework on 'selling' and 'salesmanship'. To succeed personally or in business . . . in any competitive environment, one must embrace the concept and practice salesmanship!

In the business world, a common truism is that '...nothing happens until someone sells something...' The obvious suggestion is that manufacturing, labor, all sorts of logistical support functions, taxes and consumption are triggered by a 'sale' or a transaction - and our economic system functions as a result!

On a personal level, graduates and the unemployed who knock on doors, aggressively network, and 'sell' themselves to potential employers have a serious advantage over those who send out hundreds of resumes and then sit back and wait.

Once employed, those who recognize the need to constantly 'sell' themselves and their ideas will rapidly outdistance those who function cooperatively, do everything asked, but never proactively 'sell' their ideas and talents.

The old adage, 'Good things come to those who wait' should be followed with '. . . but only those things left behind by those who hustled.'

Effective leaders are not those who say, 'Do this because I say so and I'm right' – but those who say 'Follow these practices because they are good and here's why!' If you believe in yourself, your potential and your ideas, put on your salesman's hat and convince others! Elect only leaders who passionately 'sell' their ideas!

# Security (or the appearance thereof!)

When the best strategy for protecting our homeland is asking safe, upstanding citizens take their shoes off and throw away their water bottles, while thousands of drug traffickers and illegal immigrants penetrate our borders each year, we are in deep trouble. Where has common sense gone?[138]

If the media covered the illegal immigrant threat and drug trafficking threat as extensively as they report aircraft incidents, our priorities would most certainly be redirected. If we enforced existing laws as aggressively as we defend the 'rights' of illegal immigrants, our security would be greatly enhanced.

There is a big difference between being proactive and being reactive. Our current security practices may prevent historical events from being repeated – but do nothing in anticipation of the next idea a terrorist may have. Politicians and governmental agency directors pontificate profusely (and spend billions) on their 'programs' – but every new terrorist event is a total surprise.

It doesn't take a very intelligent terrorist or illegal immigrant to observe what won't work – and, as a result, spend time thinking up new ideas. Do you think our high-budget agencies could do some 'forward-thinking' instead of spending taxpayer dollars to prevent something that won't likely be repeated? We should be looking for terrorists, not bombs! Enforce existing laws – or change them! Profile[139] – because it works!

---

[138] See **Common Sense**
[139] See **Profiling**

# Selfish Pursuits

One of the undeniable characteristics of capitalism is the presence of motivated individuals willing to take risks in order to achieve above average results. This is the definition of entrepreneurship – without which our society would not be what it is today. While this concept is demonized by socialistic-leaning idealists, our current quality of life is the result. Pure capitalism is one of those natural laws essential to maintaining our societal standards.

If we allow other misguided ideologies to erode, modify, or change these principles, everyone will be dissatisfied before long – except possibly those who have always existed by depending on the public dole.

It is essential that everyone vigorously and selfishly establish and pursue ambitious individual financial goals. Whether through frugal budgeting, creative living, and/or entrepreneurial innovation, everyone benefits when this mind-set is present.

Instead of nodding your head when demagogues suggest that successful folks should refrain from enjoying their wealth, celebrate that they have made it possible for everyone to enjoy an improved standard of living. Instead of embracing the socialistic model of wealth-sharing (which has never produced the standard of living we enjoy) vigorously demonstrate the benefits of capitalism and educate others.

When the rewards for achieving personal financial goals are restricted, growing public dependency will be the result – which is never good.

# Silence

*"You have not converted a man because you have silenced him."*
*- John Morley*

A very wise man once suggested that one cannot 'pry open a closed mind' – implying that it is often prudent to remain silent rather than challenge an obstinate individual. Remaining silent and listening [140] is often more productive than responding with premature thoughts or responses that could improve with time.

Often, those throwing out absurd ideas are also silenced when unchallenged – leading to even more absurd ideas and eventual self-destruction. Try it!

---

[140] See **Listening**

# Simplification

*"Great leaders are almost always great simplifiers,
who cut through argument and doubt to offer a solution
everybody can understand and remember."*
*- Michael Korda*

Isn't it amazing that truly great leaders often answer a question with 'yes' or 'no' – when typical politicians use up 110% of their allocated time to expound on marginally-related details?

The theory of this book is, among other things, an attempt to simplify that which is simple – to provide shortened solutions rather than overly complicated ones. We do not need new legislation to solve problems already covered by existing laws. We do not need lengthy 'investigations' to reveal what is already clear. Contracts that consume hundreds of pages are counterproductive when simple contracts between folks with common sense would serve the purpose.

# Smell Test

*"Science is facts; just as houses are made of stones, so is science made of facts; but a pile of stones is not a house and a collection of facts is not necessarily science."*

*-- Henri Poincare*

Most of us have the ability to determine whether something is real, believable, or ethical using our innate judgment and common sense. While the phrase is admittedly an idiomatic phrase - we should all understand what it means. It is another way of saying, 'That doesn't sound right', or 'It sounds too good to be true!'

Those who don't have this innate sense of judgment and common sense are those who defend the indefensible and those intellectually incoherent individuals who want 'proof' that even the most ludicrous propositions are false. We find these individuals in all walks of life - but most obviously in politics and government.

Offering excuses that don't make sense, delaying decisions under the pretense of 'investigating-further' and denying knowledge of issues that one could not possibly be unaware of . . . are examples of behaviors that simply don't pass the 'smell test'. These individuals don't have sufficient common sense to function. Avoid these folks. . and certainly don't elect or hire them!

Just because you hear something on television or read it in print, does not indicate credibility or accuracy. Determine the source, compare the information with your experience(s), and investigate further if it will impact your personal or business activities. Apply the smell test. Use your intelligence to draw a conclusion.

*It's NOT that complex!*

# Solutions

*"There is always a well-known solution to every human problem
-neat, plausible, and wrong."*
*- H. L. Mencken*

The exercise of common sense is truly becoming a lost art . . . due to distrust, beliefs not based on facts, and dishonesty.

By definition, common sense is the rational, reasoning ability given to all human beings. Cultural forces, however, are eroding this ability through a bombardment of specious statements, ulterior motives and downright falsehoods - often distributed through the popular media.[141]

Simple solutions to problems are therefore overlooked or rejected simply because they do not appear to be elaborate or expensive enough. We should strive for simplification[142] – not complexity!

---

[141] See **Stupidity**
[142] See **Simplification**

# Specious Statements

*Benford's Law of Controversy: Passion in any argument is inversely proportional to the amount of real information advanced.*

Ah . . . the art of deceptive speechmaking that is so common today!

Specious statements are those that sound plausible, sound sincere, sound believable and may be passionately delivered – but are designed to mislead. Audiences listen to eloquent, fervent, passionate, enthusiastic and persuasive presentations - but many are specious at best. Clearly, elections are won, sales are made, and court cases are won because lazy folks believe every word uttered (by speakers with microphones) without questioning, examining and reaching conclusions based on their own intelligence and reasoning. Unfortunately, most folks hesitate to use the 'L' word, preferring to label lying as simply speaking deceptively.

Make no mistake - if the intent is to mislead, distort, or hide reality, then it is specious. By the deliberate omission of crucial facts, many audiences are persuaded to embrace ideologies or programs that they would abhor if completely briefed. Again, if it sounds too good to be true, it probably is!

Critically examine the information presented when you are being asked to vote, subscribe, buy or support a new candidate, concept or product – especially when the stakes are high and the consequences irreversible!

# Statistics

*"Data is not information, information is not knowledge, knowledge is not understanding, understanding is not wisdom."*
*- Clifford Stoll*

In the electronic, computerized world, no one should ever be lacking for data to support whatever position he or she wishes to promote! This obviously has a good side and a bad side.

Polls, represented to take the pulse of the people, are regularly skewed by the wording of questions. Surveys, by the way participants are invited, are designed to yield the desired result. Even census data, as innocuous as it seems, can be used in a variety of ways simply by interpretation and manipulation.

The point to be made is the need for common sense – and the need to apply the smell test [143] to everything one reads and hears. Personal analysis is always required to intelligently react to data presented. Salesmen, politicians and other leaders regularly use 'data' to sell their ideas and make their arguments. Needless to say, they will use only the data that supports their position!

Make sure you use common sense and your personal intelligence to analyze the data you hear – and consider the source of all interpretive information based on that data!

*"Information is, above all, a principle of economy. The fewer data needed, the better the information. An overload of information leads to information blackout. It does not enrich, but impoverishes."*
*- Peter F. Drucker*

---

[143] See **Smell Test**

# Stupidity

*"Definition of Stupid:*
*Knowing the truth, seeing the truth, but still believing the lies."*
*- www.livelifehappy.com*

*"I am patient with stupidity but not with those who are proud of it."*
*- Edith Sitwell*

In defining 'common sense', we describe the basic knowledge that most people inherently possess without the benefit of formal education. It would also stand to reason that age should add volumes to one's inventory of 'common sense' – based on personal experiences and events. As adults, the ability to reason, analyze situations and make prudent decisions should be a common trait.

How then, do we explain the poor decisions so many folks make in the normal course of daily life? Common sense allows the rational analysis of problems. If egos, ulterior motives and emotions can be dismissed, or at least minimized, good outcomes can prevail.

*"Egotism is the anesthetic that dulls the pain of stupidity."*
*- Frank Leahy*

# Success

*"It is no use saying, 'We are doing our best.'*
*You have got to succeed in doing what is necessary"*
*- Sir Winston Churchill*

There are many ways to define success . . . one important thing is to define success in terms of results – not in terms of efforts. A salesman is not successful simply because he works hard or makes more calls than anyone else, he is successful when he 'sells' something! Results can be defined in terms of numbers, timing, accomplishment, peace of mind, or happiness – and we can each have different criteria. Some prefer to discuss the 'journey' rather than the 'destination'.

Truly productive folks usually set high expectations for themselves and pursue them vigorously. Truly successful people are happy while doing such!

*"The secret to success is not dreaming . . . it is doing."*
*- Leonard M Mack II*

# Supply & Demand

Supply and demand is a fundamental concept in a market economy. It is one of those natural laws![144] Attempts to introduce a better concept by regulation, price controls, restricting competition, and/or governmental supports have always failed.

In a free market economy, prices - established by the law of supply and demand - are wonderfully self-regulating. If there is a single supplier or only a handful of suppliers of a given product, and they begin raising prices unnecessarily, competition is automatically invited to compete. When a new competitor introduces a product or service at a lower price, everyone's prices fall to meet it. Assuming the product can be produced profitably at the lower price, everyone benefits!

When prices fall to the point of marginal profitability for one or more of the suppliers, the optimum price point is established. This is the fundamental basis for the free enterprise system!

---

[144] See **Natural Laws**

# Taxes

*"Income tax returns are the most imaginative fiction
being written today. "*
*-- Herman Wou*

The reason the rich don't pay taxes is because they hire experts to find loopholes. The reason the poor don't pay taxes is because bureaucrats get votes by exempting them! Let's face it - no income tax plan will satisfy everyone. Any change will temporarily upset one group or another. However, short of replacing the income tax with another means of filling the treasury, the 'flat tax' concept is, by far, the simplest, fairest, most economical and most practical.

The flat tax, where everyone pays exactly the same percentage on ALL income, with NO exemptions, is fair, painless and eliminates thousands of ambiguous rules and regulations that take thousands of IRS employees to monitor, interpret, and enforce. Even the lowest income households utilize the services provided by government and should not be exempt from paying their fair share.

To be complete, this mandate must only raise sufficient funds to meet a balanced 'budget',[145] approved *by those governed!*

Regarding exemptions, most are designed to artificially promote issues which can better be handled by the laws of supply and demand[146] or the free market system! Coupled with a reduction of government overhead and waste, most everyone, except those who currently pay *no* income taxes, would likely experience a reduction in total taxes paid.

---

[145] See **Budgets**
[146] See **Supply and Demand**

# Transparency

*"A basic tenet of a healthy democracy is open dialogue and transparency."*

*- Peter Fenn*

Let's make it even stronger. Transparency is an absolute requirement for a democracy to be healthy. There are almost no legitimate reasons for any public governing entity to hold meetings behind closed doors. The fact is that 99% of the time, such meetings are designed to hide embarrassing discussions, bad decision-making and/or incompetence on the part of the participants.

When a candidate pledges 'transparency' and promises to conduct his activities in the open, make sure he or she delivers on this promise. When excuses flow for 'executive sessions' during the legislative process, you can be assured that someone is hiding something. Obviously, military activities and national security do depend on a certain amount of confidential activity – but almost nothing else!

# Truth

*"The truth needs so little rehearsal."*
*-Barbara Kingsolver*

No one has a memory good enough to tell a lie. If one tells an untruth, sooner or later the truth will be known – and damage done. Whether on the basis of common sense, religious beliefs, or simple practical experience, telling the truth is an essential personal value that is held by responsible, mature adults.

As stated in the 'Actions Speak Louder Than Words' chapter, would you live with someone, marry someone, or hire someone that practiced deceptive behavior or language regularly and repeatedly?

Within our legal system, countless resources are wasted determining 'shades' of truth; burying un-provable lies; paying experts to extract the 'truth' and hiding 'truths' that weren't discovered according to the rules. Sadly, we also pay lots of money to legal practitioners to manipulate the truth in many cases.

If you vote for someone, work for someone, or are friends with someone that is deceptive and has no respect for the truth, make a change! Expose the deceptive behavior and untruthful words; get a new work environment or find a new friend!

It's called 'raising your standards'!

*"The most dangerous of all falsehoods is a slightly distorted truth."*
*- Georg Christoph Lichtenberg*

# I 'Understand'

What someone 'says' verbally and what is 'heard' by another is often very different. One phrase that often contributes to serious misunderstandings is the expression, *'...I understand...'*

All too often, particularly in emotion-filled moments, person 'A' will tell a story, relate an incident, or express strong feelings about something. Person 'B' will say 'I Understand' while nodding his or her head. Person 'B' meant to convey the thought 'I hear what you are saying' but what person 'A' heard was 'I approve of what you are saying and/or doing'.

As a consequence, person 'A' believes that what they have done or expressed is rational, correct, fully supported, and approved-of by person 'B'. While approval may be the intent, all too often, 'I understand' means 'I hear you - and even though I think you are totally wrong . . . but I am not going to confront you with my honest thoughts right now'.

Do everyone a favor - clearly say what you mean. Make sure you don't convey erroneous messages - particularly messages that may be misinterpreted and turn out to render unhealthy advice!!

# Unemployment

Being unemployed, through no personal fault, is devastating on many levels - emotionally, financially, professionally etc. It's not uncommon that, after many years of successful employment, many find themselves victims of changing technologies, different economic conditions and variable personnel requirements – and without a job. Many of these trends and changes were very difficult to predict for all but the top industry specialists.

Aggressively seeking employment is a full-time 'job' by itself. Delegating the task to headhunters, employment agencies and others is not, by itself, the best strategy. Simply mailing resumes and waiting for responses is not optimizing the process either. Changing one's status from 'unemployed' to 'employed' as rapidly as possible requires unrestrained energy, creativity, networking and open mindedness. Keep in mind that, for every job opening, there are probably multiple qualified candidates. Your challenge is to be the one selected.

At the risk of over-simplifying the process, your task is to convince the employer that you are the best candidate; that you will bring the most value to the firm; that you have an excellent attitude; and that you will make them glad they selected you!

There is another old adage - *'Good things come to those who wait - but only those things left behind by those who hustle!'*

# Unions

*"The only reason for a union to exist today is when employees cannot trust management."*

*- author*

Fundamentally, our society has developed into a distrusting, skeptical and doubtful group when it comes to government agencies and employers. Due to many of the concepts discussed in this book including Entitlement, Rights vs. Responsibilities, Leadership, drinking the Kool-Aid, and Specious Statements, many workers have abandoned their individual potential for self-determination and succumbed to becoming mindless 'followers'. Labor unions have capitalized on this state of affairs.

Most of the legitimate reasons unions were created (workplace conditions, safety, low wages, etc.) are very adequately controlled today by our competitive environment, labor laws and industry regulations. Management is further incentivized to treat employees properly due to competitive marketplace conditions – not only for the reputations of their products and services but the competitive nature of attracting workers!

The bad news is that the majority of labor unions today still use intimidation, confrontation, hostility, specious rhetoric and a total lack of business principles in dealing, believe it or not, with *both* management and their own members! The phony techniques of union leaders rival those of our best political campaigners!

Unions prefer that ballots not be secret, (contrary to fundamental American principles) further encouraging intimidation and coercion practices to prevail. Unions often insist on financial packages that are impossible for a company to deliver and still operate profitably.[147] Unions regularly use misleading arguments to persuade members to support disastrous ideologies at the peril of their own income. Unions often advise members to participate in behaviors detrimental to their employers' profitability (and subsequently detrimental to employees earning potential) in an effort to 'force' a given issue. The evolution of labor laws and union regulations have led to an environment today where the majority of union members were never given a chance to vote for or against a union or decide whether to join or not.

The concepts of 'cooperation' and 'mutual benefit' are, unfortunately, not objectives of most unions despite the rhetoric put forth. A lack of sensitivity to an enterprise even surviving, let alone operating profitably, is downright shortsighted. As we are seeing, particularly in some public employees' unions, some contracts' retirement benefits will bankrupt their employers if unchanged. Public employee unions are threatening the health and continued sustainability of some cities and states. Of course, bankruptcy means both management *and* members lose *everything.*

Because of the law of supply and demand and the free enterprise system that governs our economy, the best long term solutions are the simplest ones – those natural laws[148] that we cannot change. These natural laws do not need labor unions to function.

---

[147] See **Budgets**
[148] See **Natural Laws**

151

# Value

Salesmen have known for years how to sell 'value' vs. selling 'price'. Sophisticated buyers know how to evaluate products and services based on 'total cost' – and not just initial acquisition costs.

Why is it then that we are so prone to define the 'cost' of a program in terms of the cash it requires, and not the 'value' obtained? The 'bidding' process, so prevalent in corporate and governmental purchasing further promotes this misunderstanding.

A wise professor of mine once said, 'Every decision in business should be based on the economics of the situation – no other criteria'. Of course, what he was advocating was value received for resources expended – NOT the amount of cash required. The younger generation today has a hard time understanding that the 'price' of something is not always the total 'cost' or reflective of its value.

When automatically purchasing a product or service from the lowest-price vendor, something should be added for the risks that likely accompany such a decision.

# Values

*...Important and enduring beliefs or ideals shared by the members of a culture about what is good or desirable and what is not. Values exert major influence on the behavior of an individual and serve as broad guidelines in all situations....*

It should be apparent, from the actions[149] of our leaders, what their personal values are. What is perceived as important vs. unimportant is demonstrated clearly by what they do – not what they say.

Having said that, it is important that we, as constituents, make sure our values are well defined – because our actions are also an indication of our values. Before we devote precious time to campaigning for an issue, crusading for a cause or supporting a candidate, we must prioritize our values.

The source(s) of our individual values, right or wrong, originate with our upbringing, our faith, our education and the influences present in our adult life. It is important that we form our values – like our belief system[150] - based on the intelligent analysis of everything we experience and not just mass media messages or messages from our coworkers, union or spouse.

A recommitment to values can redirect this country!

---

[149] See **Actions Speak Louder than Words**
[150] See **Belief Systems**

# Vision

*"Every person takes the limits of their own field of vision
for the limits of the world."*
**-- Arthur Schopenhauer**

Vision statements have been a popular corporate mantra for some time – some seriously implemented organization-wide, while others are given lip service and then ignored.

When a vision is understood by all participants, and vigorously defended by all – truly amazing things can happen. If the leadership of an organization is absolutely committed to the vision, and 'walks the walk', success is assured.

Personal visions are a predictor of happiness and a purposeful life – and worthy of considerable personal time and energy.

# Voters

*"One of the penalties of not participating in politics is that you will be governed by your inferiors."*
*- Plato*

In high school, my government teacher advocated that '. . . not everyone should vote. . .' Of course, most of the students were appalled by this statement – and argued against his position.

In recent elections, however, it became painfully obvious that profiling[151] was used to identify certain classes of non-voters that could be 'recruited' to vote . . . benefiting a specific party. This manipulation of the system is further evidence of (a) the hypocrisy practiced by political candidates . . . that profiling is 'bad' unless utilized to benefit selfish interests and (b) the fact that not everyone should vote.

Further, requiring voter identification reduces voter fraud and is no more illegal or racist than requiring identification to fly or drive!

Voting should be the culmination of study, consideration, objective thought and intelligent judgment – not an act performed as the follow-up to a political speech or rally. The commonly heard rhetoric and specious statements during campaigns particularly persuade those who chose not to do their homework and make emotional rather than objective decisions.

The first level of active citizenship is to responsibly prepare for voting by deliberate study and intelligent observation. The second is to campaign responsibly for issues and for candidates who exhibit honesty, intelligence *and* common sense.

---

[151] See *Profiling*

# War

*"War is the greatest plague that can affect humanity;
it destroys religion, it destroys states, it destroys families.
Any scourge is preferable to it."*
                                            *-- Martin Luther*

I'm a pacifist. I hate war and killing – so don't read from this chapter that I am advocating war. However, the current concept of 'war' as practiced by our leaders is an absolute outrage.

If the cause is legitimate and the objective defined, a rational leader enters a war with his biggest weapon. He declares war, gives the other side an opportunity to surrender, and then uses every resource available as rapidly as possible to achieve that objective. The goal should be to minimize casualties on *our* side. He doesn't restrict his troops or impose 'be nice' rules. When surrender occurs, he takes the spoils and rebuilds his new territory.

If we are threatened by someone, our choice is to isolate ourselves and defend our borders *or* destroy the other party where he sits. Conflicts that arise out of ideological and cultural differences that escalate into armed conflicts are lose-lose propositions because, historically, no one ever wins. Even where protecting human rights is the only objective, winning is rare because the definition of 'human rights' is deeply ingrained by local cultural definitions.

When we're involved in a war with no clearly defined objective, no viable strategy, and no commitment to winning, leadership is obviously absent. It is expensive in terms of lives and dollars . . . and it never achieves any goal. We know this from history and we know it hasn't changed. As in any endeavor, if it's worth doing, it's worth doing right!

# Waste, Fraud & Abuse

*"The meltdown of the welfare state that we're witnessing is the ultimate justice being dealt out to those who ignore the iron laws of arithmetic."*
*- Alan Harding*

Inefficiency in government is out of control. Legislators spend far more time campaigning and posturing[152] than working hard at the important tasks at hand. Their priorities are most often established by the media, lobbyists, their own career objectives and the pursuit of personal financial gain. When their only motivation for honest, ethical behavior is the likelihood of being 'caught', and that risk is slim, ethical behavior evaporates.

Waste is evident in countless programs that benefit only special interest groups. Fraud is rampant as cited regularly by the GAO, CBO and other governmental internal auditors and watchdog agencies. Earmarks are an example of obvious abuse. Outdated, unnecessary, duplicate and ineffective programs should be eliminated. Many programs can be better performed by the private sector; and many others by state and local governments.

The excuses made for not implementing a functioning balanced budget are criminal! It's no wonder that privatization[153] seems the only solution for many problem programs. Legislators seem totally unable to wrap their heads around the concept that waste can be controlled; fraud should be prosecuted at all levels, and abuses are unethical!

---

[152] See **Posturing**
[153] See **Privatization**

# Wealth

*"Earning and knowing how to keep your own wealth
does not guarantee happiness, but the absence of it
will guarantee your misery"*
    *- Dick Purdum*

Someone wise once said, '…wealth is when small efforts produce
large results. Poverty is when large efforts produce small
results…' Our current educational system, our family –based
culture and even our leaders do not stress enough the role personal
wealth pursuits should take in our lives.

Everyone should make it a priority to identify wealth objectives
and work daily to develop and protect their individual assets. One
observation to make is the relatively low level of 'savings' held by
our citizenry as compared to those in other countries. Another is
the attitudes towards instant gratification and entitlement prevalent
on all levels of our society.

We'd all be better off studying the historical basis for the wealth of
those at the top segment of our society and learn from them.


It's ***not*** that complex!

www.ingramcontent.com/pod-product-compliance
Lightning Source LLC
Chambersburg PA
CBHW060859280326
41934CB00007B/1120